A Beginner's Guide to America

A Beginner's Guide to America

FOR THE IMMIGRANT AND THE CURIOUS

ROYA HAKAKIAN

Alfred A. Knopf

NEW YORK   2021

THIS IS A BORZOI BOOK
PUBLISHED BY ALFRED A. KNOPF

Published in the United States by Alfred A. Knopf,
a division of Penguin Random House LLC,
New York, and distributed in Canada
by Penguin Random House Canada Limited, Toronto.

www.aaknopf.com

Knopf, Borzoi Books, and the colophon are registered
trademarks of Penguin Random House LLC.

Library of Congress Cataloging-in-Publication Data
Names: Ḥakkākiyān, Ru'yā, author.
Title: A beginner's guide to America : for the immigrant and the curious /
Roya Hakakian.
Description: New York : Alfred A. Knopf, 2021.
Identifiers: LCCN 2020016857 (print) | LCCN 2020016858 (ebook) |
ISBN 9780525656067 (hardcover) | ISBN 9780525656074 (ebook)
Subjects: LCSH: Immigrants—United States—Handbooks, manuals, etc. |
Immigrants—United States—Life skills guides. | United
States—Emigration and immigration—Handbooks, manuals, etc.
Classification: LCC JV6543.H34 2021 (print) | LCC JV6543 (ebook) |
DDC 646.70086/9120973—dc23
LC record available at https://lccn.loc.gov/2020016857
LC ebook record available at https://lccn.loc.gov/2020016858

Jacket photograph by Flavia Mortachetti / Moment / Getty Images
Jacket design by Jenny Carrow

Manufactured in the United States of America
First Edition

In memory of my father,
the first Hakakian to write,
the last Hakakian to arrive in America

So Odysseus, with tact,
said, "Do not be enraged at me, great goddess.
You are right. I know my modest wife
Penelope could never match your beauty.
She is human; you are deathless, ageless,
But even so, I want to go back home . . ."

—Homer, *The Odyssey,* translated by Emily Wilson

* * *

I love America more than any other country in the world,
and, exactly for this reason, I insist on the right to criticize her
perpetually.

—James Baldwin, *Notes of a Native Son*

* * *

I'd better get right down to the job.
It's true I don't want to join the Army or turn lathes in precision
parts factories, I'm nearsighted and psychopathic anyway.
America I'm putting my queer shoulder to the wheel.

—Allen Ginsberg, "America"

Contents

Prologue

In August 1984, I fled my beloved homeland, Iran. After many months of wandering through Europe as a refugee, I was finally admitted into the United States. What I say in this book is what no one told me when I first arrived, when all I heard was about practicalities, and nothing about how to understand or cope with the whirlwind of emotions that had swept me up and in whose eye I remained for a long time. Everyone was trying to help me get on with my new life, all the while I was under the sad spell of the old.

No two immigrants are the same, therefore no two arrival experiences are the same. Yet even as immigrant groups are divided based on their strengths or shortcomings, successes or failures in America, they have far more in common as members of an uprooted community, trying to make their way in the unfamiliar land. This book is, in part, about all that bonds them. Immigrants are not interchangeable. And yet, just as there are common human experiences, there are also common immigrant experiences. Scholars, for their own scientific purposes, and politicians, for their own partisan purposes, often focus on immigrants as distinctly separate groups to measure their value to, or their burden on, the nation, to debate which one should be allowed in and which should be banned altogether. In truth, all that separates one group from another often pales against the common drama of displacement and the ordeal of resettlement. Speaking of that drama is one way of warding off those who wish to reduce the shared narrative of that odyssey to a series of disjointed entries in the encyclopedia of arrival.

In offering the newcomer's perspective, this book will inevitably cast a fresh look at America, rethinking and presenting her to all readers through the weathered perspective of a naturalized citizen. Perhaps those who have been born and raised here, and assume that their mere birth either endows them with the knowledge of America or exempts them from exploring and discovering her, can see her anew, through the eyes of others who dream of becoming Americans.

Much of what follows is the story of my own life, and the lives of people I love or have tried to help in a personal or professional capacity. If there is an attempt, it is at inclusivity, at trying to weave in as many immigrant experiences as would fit the confines of these pages. In the end, I was left with an unusual composition made up of my own recollections and those of my fellow immigrants as told in memoirs, autobiographies, personal testimonies, and other thoughtful and provocative writings on the subject, which I have listed in my sources. The result is part memoir, part reportage, and part a work of imagination. True to the nature of displacement, this book has elements of all these genres, but ultimately belongs to none of them. My greatest hope has been to give an unmediated access to a narrative that has become disfigured by overzealous emissaries on both sides of the political debate.

I have lived through war and a violent revolution. I have been persecuted for my religion, gender, and beliefs, too. What I hope all these experiences bring to this book is a measure of authenticity. Authenticity is not all an immigrant needs, but it is a good place to begin a new conversation, or a new book.

Roya Hakakian
October 2020

PART I

ONE

Upon Arrival in America the Beautiful

A newcomer can do much to teach himself—especially if
he is not afraid of being called a "greenhorn."

—MARIAN SCHIBSBY, *Handbook for Immigrants to the United States,*
FOREIGN LANGUAGE INFORMATION SERVICE (1927)

The long-awaited day is here. You are almost in America. Up
in the sky, you press your forehead against the glass and look
down. There you see her for the first time. If you are arriving
at night, America, the jewel, shimmers beneath. If in daytime,
you see the outlines of her riches, the green of her lush woods,
the blue of her leviathan waters. Until then, you had only felt
exhaustion and sleeplessness. But all that vanished at the first
glimpse of the ground. Now there is only fear and excitement
coursing through you.

It has been a long time since you have been welcomed anywhere. Tears—of dread, sadness, or gratitude, you cannot be
sure—blur your view of the forms you must fill out before landing. If you come from a country of compulsory dress codes—

veils, scarves, or niqabs—you might shed the layers now, but remember that soon customs officers will glance at the photograph in your passport and then at you standing before them to reconcile the two versions of you. This is the first of many masks you will shed in the years to come.

From the moment you step off the plane, your eyes will search for the traces of Americanness in your surroundings. Yet the sun is the same sun. The asphalt looks just as black. The jetway gives the same groan all other jetways give underfoot. The transit corridors lit with fluorescent lights stretch as menacingly as all passageways you have gone through. Only when you stand in line—one hand clutching a bag, another on the handle of a suitcase—and your eyes begin to rove about will you see something you have only seen at a tourist destination before. Pinned on the flap of the chest pockets of the officers guiding everyone are name tags—"Sanchez," "McWilliams," "Cho," "Al-Hamed"—and, by God, all of them Americans! If jet lag has not clouded your senses, you will instantly recognize this to be the surest sign of America. In the monochrome life you just left behind, such a motley human landscape would have been unthinkable.

FIRST INSPECTIONS

At the reception hall of the terminal, there will be lots of activity, and great, exhausted crowds will teem about you. But there will be none of the alarming chaos that had come with the crowds of the past. When it is your turn in line, you will be called to a booth. There are more forms to fill out. You will present your pleasantest self through the glass, while anxiety boils inside. If you are lucky, the officer will look up with a smile and say, "Welcome to America!" Then the floodgates of tears you had worked so hard to push back will open again, and you will weep. Weeping is the last thing you want to do at your first meeting in the new country, but you cannot help it. No one will ask why you cry. The officer knows, as do you, that though America is not yet your home, it is the place where you have come to breathe, find peace, and rest at last.

If you are not lucky—for this is where you could be detained or even turned back—you will reach the booth of a moody officer who will only ask for your passport. You offer it reverently, in the palms of both hands, like a sacrifice at an altar. With every leaf he turns, your heart beats faster. You are ready to be suspected, interrogated for your "country of origin." Sweat beads on your temples. Nothing good ever came of a uniform where you used to live. Uniforms belonged to the powerful. They were the people you had to outfox. Here you must do your best to remember that the officers in the booths have little in common with the ones you used to fear. Take deep breaths and remind yourself that you are in a place where the law, for the most part, is king.

You are waiting for a stamp in your passport, the nine-digit numeric benediction that launches millions from everywhere to enter into the green card lottery. The card you will get in a year will primarily be white, and it will bear this very number. Roughly 3½ by 2 inches, it will allow you to cross from an uncertain life over which you had no control to an uncertain life that will be of your making—to a preferable form of uncertainty. The card will have your essential coordinates: birth date, signature, full name, photo, and thumbprint. The latter bears the crass sign of a mark branded on cattle, but no matter. You will be a "resident alien," able to live and work in the United States, though for the foreseeable future you will feel the alien far more acutely than the resident. Your color portrait in the foreground will be to the left of that of Lady Liberty in the background. You and she, your timid smile beside her regal crown, will be a pair. Your once-distant dream will soon be real and laminated.

Dogs will come around to sniff your bags. Officers will rummage through your belongings, wrinkling their noses at the scent of your spices. The younger ones among them might sneer at your traditional pantsuit, your meticulously translated bundle of transcripts or certificates of merit and awards, your lovingly folded stack of sashes and ribbons, reminders of past glories that duly fill you with pride. They will undo them, then toss them onto a jumbled heap. This is how America welcomes everyone: by preparing them for anonymity. Gird yourself for what you will surely register as disrespect, a personal offense, yet it is merely disregard for what you have achieved elsewhere. America cares little about what you have done, only what you will do while you are here. This is the first of many times your heritage will be tossed aside. But they will not take away your books, or examine the writings in your journals, or ban you from speaking or publishing what you choose.

You will gather your suitcases bursting with all that you

could salvage of your old life. Your mind, too, is bursting with all that you have been told about America. Keep the suitcases, but discard the knowledge. In fact, even before going through the last set of metal detectors to get on a plane to your final destination, place your views of America—along with your shoes, keys, coins, and cell phone—in the gray rubber bins, and leave them there. What you know is likely to be a distortion—not without truth, but without precision. It always takes months, if not years, to sift through all that one has hauled across the continents and decide what to keep and what to scrap. The sermons about America that angry imam delivered at Friday prayers, the tirade the principal shouted over the bullhorn in the schoolyard at the queues of pupils, or the rants the talk show hosts broadcast on state-run television cannot guide you through the real America. You will receive many gifts during your time here, but the greatest of them all is America herself, lying before you beyond the revolving doors of the airport. She will surely break your heart, but the heartbreaks, like the joys, are not in the scripts you have been handed. The sooner you part with the old inherited notions, the faster you will navigate your way through the thicket of your new life. And this is the first day of that new life, a second birth of sorts. The day of your arrival will someday become a major date in your calendar. It will be neither public like the Fourth of July or New Year's Day, nor festive like a birthday, but it will give you an annual pause and you will look back tenderly at yourself and at this very moment, standing on the street, breathing the air of a new world.

STEPPING ONTO THE AMERICAN STREET

When you step onto the street for the first time, an awestruck feeling will wash over you. You will be exhausted but alert, too. What you will see then will remain with you in the same way that your wedding day, first day of school, or the birth of a child will always remain with you. Years from now, people will ask you to tell your memories of this day. What you will recall will hardly be about the things before your eyes, but the feelings the views conjured in you. Tourists look at, pose beside, and take photographs of what they see. The uprooted observe and contemplate the significance of those views.

The things you hear will equally stay with you. You will find the air thick with noises you have not heard in a long time, or have simply never heard before. In the past when you thought of freedom, you thought of free speech as its only sound. But sometimes freedom's best trace is not in words but in silence. It is in the absence of the whispers that fear spreads. It rings in the humming of a teenage boy, standing in the bus line, swaying to the uncensored music in his ear; in the swishing of a carefree teenage girl, gliding past on roller skates; in the unafraid laughter of two women chattering; in the whistling of a dreamy security guard; in the unprohibited tunes that waft out of the passing cars; in the barking of full-bellied pet dogs, not banned by any edicts, cockily walking at the side of their owners; or in the stilted yet civil uttering of the shopkeepers' "Can I help you?" (for business is the daytime god and must go on despite all else); in every tapping foot or clapping hand that does as instinct commands; in all the ways that a people who have not been cowed into silence exercise their sonorous existence.

Seeing the size of the cars and the people, you will wonder if you have arrived in the land of giants. The landscape before you is vast. There seems to be no end to what you see. The sky, the avenues, the buildings go on and on and on. Your neck will stretch more than it ever has when you tilt your head back to see the top of a skyscraper. You will not hesitate to fill your lungs with the translucent air. If you come from a land where women must don the veil, you will be stunned to see veil-less women walk about. You will be even more stunned to see a few veiled ones passing them by, each paying no mind to the other. The two versions of Eve you thought could never mix are milling about before your very eyes. This is another American miracle, not only of harmony among ethnicities but also beliefs.

If you, yourself, donned the veil, not by personal choice but by religious order, here is your chance to peel it away, give your head a good shake, and let the wind blow through your hair. What will be even more wondrous than your bare head is that no one will stare at you, and unlike what the clerics had always warned, no men will be driven wild. In fact, you will be disappointed at how uneventful it is to be bareheaded. America has a veil of her own—the cloak of insignificance—that she instantly drapes over everyone. All you had been told about the dangers of veil-lessness proves untrue. The only one staring at that moment is you, at the oblivious passersby. For so long, you lived under the gaze of neighbors, intelligence agents, or male family members whose business it was to guard your "virtue." On the streets you knew, people held a ceaseless vigil, monitoring the block. Neighbors were often busybodies who watched the comings and goings of other neighbors. Stricken men and women whose lives had been brought to a standstill by war, tyranny, or disaster sat on their stoops, at their windows, and ogled. Perhaps they were waiting for the blight over their lives to lift like fog, or for the savior to arrive. Those who gawked did so on behalf of the authorities, or fearing them. Newspapers report on how bombings, autocrats, or typhoons ruin economies and spread disease. Charts and graphs, with numbers lined in columns next to them, show the rise and fall of the GDP, air quality, human health. But the more commonplace fallouts of tyranny, as they affect life's ordinary routines, are less measurable. Apathy, evil in its own way, is a luxury of freedom. At the voting booth, democracy boils down to a ballot. On ordinary streets, as you see them on that first day, it manifests as indifference. The novelty you are experiencing today is just that. No one watches or cares much about what you do as long as you do not harm anyone. Bask in the icy calm of this refreshing indifference. Years later, you might yearn for attention. But for now, you want to vanish amid the crowd and find this oblivion comforting.

THE ROAD TO YOUR DESTINATION

The relatively clean sidewalks might escape you on that first day, but if you do notice them, they will make you pause. There will be a breeze, yet little trash to swirl along the ground. In time, you will wonder about the cleanliness of the streets, and the reasons why your old streets were strewn with litter and these streets are not. However, now is not the time for such ruminations. You must find your way home.

You get into your taxi and are surprised to see that you are its only passenger. There is no one else around to squeeze you against the door, to make room for. Though you can spread out, you will keep your body compact within the humble boundaries of past cab rides. But in time the vastness of America will inspire you to sprawl, too, and to grow into your new roomier surroundings. As your taxi pulls away from the curb, either your driver or an incessant beeping will force you to put on your seat belt. Since you are not accustomed to observing any safety practices, the seat belt will cause you to feel bound as if in a straitjacket. The thought of having such protection only to ride through peaceful streets is laughable to you. Car crashes were the least of your worries in the land you left behind, a place where the living were not so protected, the sirens of aerial bombings, or all manner of violence, were as common as church bells in the small towns of America. Sometimes you were treated as a human ATM at manned roadblocks on lawless streets, handing out cash to thugs or the adolescent gang members who were the self-appointed gatekeepers of your town. Now you only worry about a mere accident. Even though you already feel the safest you have ever felt, you must put on your seat belt, for it is the law, as are helmets for cyclists. These safety measures make you realize, better than any seal or stamp in your passport, that you have officially moved into a territory where human life is not as cheap as you once knew.

For the first few minutes of the drive, you will be mostly dizzy, watching layers of iron and cement pass overhead, criss-crossing the air, dizzier yet when you realize that all the cars, tailgating in traffic, make so few sounds. So little honking! Much of the public frustration in your former homeland was aired on the congested streets. Anger at the authorities and their oppressive ways found its safest outlet behind the wheel of a car among the legions of fellow irate drivers. It was always in a gridlock that your countrymen could best object to the arbitrary rules they had been forced to live under, and they used honking and cussing as a form of mischanneled protest. Dis-obeying traffic laws, watching the helpless policeman toot and signal to no avail, was the closest they got to avenging them-selves on their bad leaders.

On the highway, you will read every sign you pass by. All the names—Franklin, Pleasantville, Long Beach—are equally unfamiliar to you. North, south, east, and west are no longer directions, only reminders that this is not home, and these arrows will not take you to any place where someone is waiting for you. Melancholy will now stalk you, and you must resist it however you can, even if simply by distracting yourself. Notice the other signs? Some of them you have seen before—yield, pedestrian crossing, slow down—others you have not: *This por-tion of the highway was adopted by* . . . You ask your driver what the sign says. When he explains the meaning, you realize that a swath of asphalt here is looked after better than some of the living things in your former homeland.

Out of the city en route to your destination in the quieter

parts, you might see a river or a lake along the road. It is not likely that water has been part of your daily scenery. That is why you wonder whether he is driving you to the beach. But soon you will learn that bays, lakes, oceans, rivers, and the rest, bodies of water whose names have yet to enter your arid lexicon, are part of this landscape. At the first sighting of woods, you might think you have stumbled upon a rare patch for a hike or picnic. But then you will go farther and see that these forests are endless and, indeed, you have come to the birthplace of verdant things. Where your eyes expect to see brown and gray, you will mostly find variations of blue and green. Such small miracles are at their most visible in those early days, when you are at your most vulnerable and certainty is at a premium—the past is not yet bygone and the future is not yet guaranteed. Commit these wonders to memory. Soon you will think of them as your personal entitlements and take them for granted.

AN EXHAUSTED FINALE

At your destination, you, if a refugee, may find that the local church has furnished your apartment, covered your beds with sheets, hung towels on the bathroom racks. Or the synagogue has lined up tutors for your children, or posted a note on your refrigerator with the name of several volunteers to drive you to where you need to go. Or the mosque has stocked your refrigerator. You wonder why, because you might not be a Jew, a Christian, or a Muslim, but those who furnished your home did not care about your religion, only that you were new in town and the latest member of their community. It will be a while until you learn that Americans have a penchant for volunteerism and "service." You will ponder these acts and may not know immediately what to do or say in return. You will not be your agile self for a long time. Watching the new world, soaking up the foreign tongue, making sense of every unexpected nod or grin, learning to walk about under the weight of a past that is viciously present will slow you down. For now, take a deep breath and rest. You are here, exhilarated and exhausted.

There was darkness and now a glimmer of light—your first day in America.

TWO

Genesis Redux

America wants people who are clean: Because clean
people do not bring sickness with them.

—CECILIA RAZOVSKY,
What Every Emigrant Should Know (1922)

There is only one way for your first night in America to end, for
all nights lead to darkness, but many ways for your first morning to begin: You might be lying in bed in the twilight of wake-
fulness, eavesdropping on the breaking day. Your ears take in
the muffled voices of the neighbors. The unfamiliar echoes will
first startle, then quickly sadden you. You realize that it is not
the remnants of sleep that keep you from making sense of the
strange sounds you hear, but that it is you—you are the stranger
now. You look around and see your open suitcase on the floor.
You feel the heft of each article inside just by looking at it.
There is so much more in every fold than the customs officers
could ever know. What will you do with your clothes? Your
warm woolen things are no match for America's bone-crushing

chill. Your light linen things will look odd here. Their style will give you away instantly as an outsider, even before you open your mouth to speak.

Your eyes linger on the lump of keys to your old home in one of the pockets of the suitcase, sharp edges jutting through the lining—you packed them not because they were necessary but because you did not have the heart to leave them behind. Of all that you brought, they are the most useless. You knew they would be but still tucked them in the suitcase. You understand that the past is past, but you keep the keys, because they can open the gates of memory. Your old house might have been bombed, or sold, or razed altogether, but its keys remain. Your passport will expire someday. Your parents will pass on. In your homeland, you will soon be forgotten. But your keys are your proof that there were once a set of locks on a door. To a house. Of a person. Of you. Your keys are your history—evidence of your old existence.

YOUR FIRST UNPLANNED ENCOUNTER

There will be a knock at the door from, let us assume, a rotund person with a tool belt around his waist. When you open the door, the words spill from his mouth like a steady stream from a faucet. Towering over you, he is all smiles, and you are all confusion. In his shirt pocket is a scroll long enough to reach his collar. Your eyes catch the word "lease" on the document, and you think this bubble of a man must be your landlord, or working for him. He has extended a hand, and when you shake it, his hand swallows yours. The size of his grip will stun you.

Here most things are, as the commercials winningly blare, *extra large*. Beware that the American "extra" is far more generously proportioned.

When he lets go of your hand, he taps his chest and enunciates a word—his name, you venture, and you introduce yourself in return. He scrawls the name on the back of a card and gives it to you. Then he will likely ask, "How's it going?" You might think this a genuine expression of interest in and concern for you and your state of affairs and will be tempted to give him a thorough briefing. You may want to tell him about the airport, the security screening, the cab ride, and your disorienting jet lag. If you do, he is likely to be confused or interrupt you. You see, the American "How's it going?" which comes in several varieties—"How are you doing?" or the curt "What's up?"—is, in fact, the equivalent of a little verbal cough to clear the throat. It is no more than a conversational lubricant to accompany a nod or handshake, not an invitation to a real dialogue. A mere "Everything is okay, and you?" will do.

The still-running faucet pauses briefly and then asks, "Where are you from?"

And there! You have arrived at the most vexing four words of your early days in America. Your reaction to this will be, above all, one of alarm. Your immediate thought will be that your pleasant manner has failed. After all, he has found you out, knows you are not from here. You take it to mean that you do not belong, and if you have a particularly gloomy nature, you worry that you can never belong. Even after years of being here, and trying to fit in, your accent, or something else about you,

will always give you away, and the question, with a minor variation can still haunt you: *Where are you really from?*

When you are new, as you are on that first morning, anxiety
explains all things before reason does. But in time, you will see
that there are as many interpretations for those four words as
there are words for snow for the Eskimo. Asking where you are
from can often simply be a way of breaking the proverbial ice.
You might say, "I'm from Thailand," to which the person asking the question could, in turn, excitedly say, "My housekeeper
is Thai" or "I love drunken noodles." You might not be fond of
your national cuisine, but no matter. "Where are you from?" is
launched into the conversation only to further the introduction.
Even the native-born ask each other the same question just to
get acquainted. Sometimes it might lead to a wistful memory:
"You're the spitting image of my cousin Matti, may he rest in
peace." Or, if the person asking is a single man or woman in
pursuit of love, the following can ensue: "If everyone in your
country looks like you, I know where I must go for my next
vacation!" Such lines are most common at watering holes and
nightclubs. However, an encounter with a freshly arrived immigrant can have a disarming effect, not unlike that of alcohol.

In truth, and especially in those early days, "Where are
you from?" is prone to cause more trouble than good. If you
come from a communist or other anti-American stronghold,
you worry that the person asking might be wondering about
your allegiances. If you come from a country in the throes of
civil strife, you fear he might suspect that you have fought on
the wrong side of the conflict. If you are from a nation with a

record of fist pumping and sword brandishing in front of televi-sion cameras—Iraq, Syria, Yemen, for example—sometimes he, wishing to confirm the place of your origin, might run his hand across his neck to sign a beheading. That is when you realize that a meat cleaver is now shorthand for your ancient civilization.

In the early days after your arrival, "Where are you from?" is, above all, a reminder of your unpreparedness to speak of the past. You have yet to shape your story—what you saw, why you left, how you left, and what it took to get here. This narrative is your personal Book of Genesis: The American Volume, the one you will sooner or later pen, in the mind if not on the page. You must take your time to do it well and to do it justice. In the midst of a dinner party, holding your wineglass just as your favorite Hollywood starlet holds hers, nodding your amiable nods, flashing the rehearsed smile of one whose lips are well accustomed to the contours of happiness, you cannot respond honestly to "Where are you from?" Amid the soft sound of jazz, the sweet scent wafting from a flickering candle, and the polite bustle of tuxedoed servers circulating bite-size delicacies on sil-ver trays, the mention of your overturned dinghy, or the weeks and months of marching to get away from your violence-ridden hometown, followed by waiting in a reeking, disease-ridden camp, or the sirens signaling aerial bombings that drove you into the shelter is, well, anticlimactic. It is also unwise if you would like to see, perhaps for the first time, what promises a deliciously dim ambience can hold. You must treat your story as a conductor often treats his orchestra, only drawing on a few instruments at a time—one tale here, another there—and in good time and with trust, perhaps you can employ the entire ensemble.

If pressed, you are better off with inexact titles like "Asian," "African," "Latina." Or sometimes you might turn to the benign and more respectable versions of your heritage. For instance, to avoid conjuring menacing ayatollahs to mind, you might not wish to call yourself Iranian. It would be better to associate yourself with lush rugs and purring cats by calling yourself Persian instead. Or if you are from Israel and fear souring a good dinner conversation by mentioning your nationality, you might simply stick to, say, Ukrainian Jew. Good ad hoc remedies can alleviate immediate stress, though they will fail you as permanent cures.

When to give the straight answer to "Where are you from?" is only half the dilemma. The other is the response that it often elicits from the person asking, which is likely to be, "You must be glad you're here." And though you *are* glad that you are here, at that moment you do not want your odyssey simply summarized and punctuated with mere gladness. Their certainty and expectation that you ought to be glad and grateful irritate you. Your instant reaction is to be unglad and ungrateful. You are fully aware how horrid were the circumstances, the land you left behind, but it was the land on whose grounds you had learned to walk, under whose sun you had warmed. *You* can denigrate that land because you and *it* are, however bitterly, inseparable. Strangers cannot. If they do, they would denigrate you, too.

But you must remember that in your tender post-arrival

state, your responses to encounters such as the one with that first imaginary visitor at your door are mostly the handiwork of unsettledness and its conjoined twin, vulnerability. You easily take offense because the statement assumes that you chose to uproot yourself. Or that even if you did not, the ultimate uprooting came painlessly. Or that you had always meant to dispose of your past, leave your ancestral home, and set yourself on a cross-continental odyssey. Or that you find it natural to be where your father is not buried and no headstone in any cemetery bears the name of your kin. Or worse yet, that whatever you may have lost has been made up for now that you are, behold, in this American one-bedroom, utilities not included. It assumes that you have either materialized from the ether, or that all you once lived with, upon touchdown at the American port, lifted like the ether. Someday "Where are you from?" will be no more important than "How's the weather today?" though this is hardly a consolation to you now.

A MOSEY IN THE NEW NEIGHBORHOOD

If you have moved into a low-rent housing district in a metropolis, you will be unimpressed by the look of this America—dirty streets, boarded-up buildings, and graffiti-riddled walls. It will have all the crime and poverty that you had expected to see anywhere but here. Stay and you run the risk of being robbed or cheated out of the precious few belongings that you have come with. Better to start your first few weeks in the suburbs or a small town. There you look out of the windows of your bedroom and see only cars where you expected to see people. If it is a mild season, when you leave your home in such a neighborhood, you will hear songs of chirping birds, see endless rows of trees and serene homes gleaming under the sun. You might even feel as if you had stepped inside a bucolic painting. It is the kind of beauty you have never known—the beauty of uneventfulness. What will get your attention are the flags hung from holders at some of the houses you pass, which strike you with a strange mix of serenity and militancy. For most other nations, the flag is something that flies over government and official buildings. For Americans, it is much more. It is how the ancestral pioneer lives on by staking a claim to the personal frontier.

None of what once caused you to fear a stroll through your old neighborhood is here. Not the random spray of a sniper's gun, not the anxiety of a lurking mine under the ground, not a bearded paramilitary figure prowling about, or plainclothes security agents. Your steps will grow more assured. You will practically bounce along—until you pass the vast dry lawn of one particular property. Suddenly a terrifying machine-gun-like rat-a-tat sounds off and you are showered with what you expect to be bullets but are, in fact, the discharged drops of water from a timed sprinkler system. For several moments, America dissolves, and your old fears hold you in their grip until you catch your breath and regain your composure.

You resume your walk. You will notice unchained and unguarded furniture on lawns and porches. Perfectly ripe edible pumpkins are left on stoops. Bundles of good corn dangle from front doors. Loose gnomes and statues dot the lawns.

Great swaths of luxuriant grass ring every home, the kind they build a public park around in your birth country, where hundreds would picnic and play. These expanses are mostly idle, except every four years, when they become an outdoor broadcast post for electoral placards and campaign signs. You should know sooner rather than later that every American surface—buildings, humans, bodies of moving vehicles, the blue heavens above—is first and foremost an aspiring billboard. Americans worship at the altar of "privacy," and yet their beliefs, upon two-sided, eighteen- by twenty-four-inch corrugated signs, wither in the sun, or are pasted on the bumpers of their cars. There are no walls here around the homes or along streets. You can watch neighbors swinging on the swings, their food smoking on their grills in the backyard. At night, lights will be on everywhere. The city will not be as bright as it is during the day, but it will be no less beautiful. Here, the only time the hum of electricity dies out, save amid a disaster, will be when you choose to turn it off.

WELCOME TO THE FREE WORLD'S WIDE WEB

Your stroll will lead you to a café, where you will open your laptop for the first time since you arrived. It is here that you will experience your first American web surfing, which will prove unforgettable. You log into your email account and the page opens instantly. You click on an email, and it pops up just as fast. You type Google, Facebook, Twitter, and, by God, you will not have to watch the hourglass turn and turn. The speed of this transfer will not be the usual slow, filtered trickle—rather a steady, unadulterated stream. Yet again, your delight might quickly turn into gloom if you wallow on thoughts of the past, and how your access was limited or how much time you lost in waiting. But these sorrows will only weigh you down at a time when you need to be at your lightest, in spirit above all.

You try Amazon. You had always heard there was an electronic super bazaar but you had not seen it for yourself. You click on "Books." You want to see the books you had always dreamed of reading but were banned or censored in your homeland. This will be your first opportunity to read the things you never could before and solve the pressing riddles of your own history. How bizarre that you had to leave your country to learn the truth about its past. You feast upon the covers of all the forbidden volumes. *Mao: The Unknown Story*. Fifty years of secrets fall away in the span of a few seconds and clicks. *The Satanic Verses*. Now that it is so available and in so many editions, it seems so much less satanic. *Fifty Shades of Grey* in all its various formats and merchandise options colorfully appears before you. *The Da Vinci Code*. Decoded. You even find an electronic copy of the Kama Sutra and scroll through its pages in the only position you never thought you would strike: seated undisturbed at a café full of patrons.

You download one of the books and delight in seeing that no words are blacked out. If you are a dissident, your new, uncensored circumstances will prove pricey, for you will click your way to your newfound freedom, ordering the titles you had never dared keep at home. It will take a while for you to believe that it is safe to carry such books in your handbag, or to be seen reading them on the train. It will take even longer until the sight of a uniformed man will not cause you palpitations.

GROCERY SHOPPING 2.0

Your next stop will be a supermarket. As you enter, you may hear cheerful welcome greetings. A worker, with his name next to a smiley face on a tag clipped to his stained apron, will approach you. Eyes wide, lips open in a grin, he will ask the most quintessential American question of all, which is also this nation's greatest contribution to the global economic discourse: "How may I help you today?" Hearing this, you will feel startled for two reasons: first, because in your birth country store staff were loath to serve customers—no one ever tipped anyway, so why bother—much less approach them to offer to do so; second, because in your former homeland only the dim-witted smiled at strangers for no good reason. Prepare to see many such smiles here. They are a common expression to help ease interaction, make a good impression, win you over as a customer, or convey what cannot be conveyed with words, where there is a language barrier. Bear in mind that there is no guarantee the American smilers are any less obtuse than those in your former homeland. There the king or president, or anyone powerful for that matter, turned his gaze away from the people and appeared grave in posters, as if the serious expression somehow lessened the chaos, corruption, or uncertainty in the country. In contrast, look at the photo of any American president and you will see him looking directly into the camera, smiling broadly. The smile is to give his supporters confidence that the bright future he promised them is on its way.

You head for the produce section to see familiar things you know and know what to do with. But these fruits will astound you. It might be the middle of December, yet the shelves are stocked with cherries, apricots, and watermelons so ripe that they might have been picked in the sunlight of June. And they, like most American things, are mammoth versions of what you are used to. An apple here will be three times the size of the apples of your past. Gleaming and curvaceous, without a flaw on their skins, these apples are not in the messy mounds you remember, specks of dirt dotting their figures. They are the apples of still-life paintings, well lit and dewy. But when you pick one up to enjoy the apple smell you love, there is no scent. Other similarly fetching fruits are scentless, too. You had come to the supermarket to find familiar sights and aromas but feel mildly betrayed by the antiseptic air reminiscent of the air of a pharmacy. This is the first of many instances when the new you encounter resembles the old, but only superficially.

You will drift into the health section of the supermarket. Here they sell all sorts of preventive remedies: pills to take to stop the pain that may come, vapors to inhale, extra-strength liquids or tablets to drink or chew in two varieties of bright day-time yellow or calming nighttime blue, ointments to rub on just in case, bands to wrap around one's limbs to prevent injury, fizzy drinks to calm an imminent upset, drops and sprays to alleviate the feeling of . . . well, feeling. All these so perfectly preempt pain that their consumers are often left feeling nothing at all. So good are these at battling discomfort that they bring on numbness, which is a mere pit stop from apathy. And if there is a single feeling America must do all she can to kick, it is apathy.

In one particular aisle, you find cans of beef, chicken, and fish priced much lower than others you had seen in previous aisles. Pleased with your find, you pile them into your cart. Then you hesitate when you see a picture of a dog or a cat on each can. You remember the feral cats and emaciated dogs that used to roam your streets. They were sometimes hunted, sometimes banned for being unclean, and always unloved. It is not until you see leashes, rubber bones, and miniature sweaters in a large bin in the same aisle, all 40 percent off, that you realize the unthinkable is true: Americans feed proper food to their pets here, and even dress them. To think that you were about to stock your cabinets with animal feed! What would your former countrymen say if they got wind of this? You can hear the wise-cracks: *He went all the way to America to eat dog food!* It will be years until you learn that pets are venerated in this country, at times even as much as, if not more than, children. For now, you gingerly put the cans back and hurry into the next aisle.

There you will be mystified once more. On shelf after shelf, you will find enough boxes to declare a republic of cereal. All your life, you had known cereal to have only one shape, color, and flavor, at the most two. It came in a smaller box than the ones before you, with only a few words written on each. As if the super-sized boxes were not enough, the many sentences make you feel there is something far more respectable than mere cereal inside. In the face of all the variety, you wonder if you really knew cereal before.

Do not let this imposing lineup crowd your vision and get in the way of seeing what transcends mere cereal. While so much variety rightly strikes you as frivolous, you must remember it is the presence of variety that matters. Simply put, the past was a black-and-white picture, and America, Technicolor. Cereal is proof that you have left the universe of Manichaean options, where you usually had to consider between bad and mediocre. (The quality of good had plummeted, since it was always all that was available.) You are in the land of choice, where you must think and select according to your own taste. Open the floodgates of inhibition. If only you could stop the comparisons, without shuttling back to that elsewhere in your mind. But this will be hard in these early days, and possibly even longer. You cannot see anything new on its own. You can only see it against the memory of the old.

THE ABCs OF AMERICAN PECULIARITIES

You turn the cereal box over and check its price: $5.99. The .99 puzzles you. Why waste three perfectly good numbers for the sake of a negligible cent? A flat $6 looks more efficient and easier to add up at the register. Upon inspection, you find that other items are similarly priced. You figure the decimal point and extra numbers must be harder to fit on the tiny price tags. But some things are inexplicable about America, these silly prices among them. They are there because marketers believe they make customers think they are paying less. Marketers are also the purveyors of other absurdities and euphemisms such as "Buy more and save!" Marketers are the reason you will soon begin to frown every time the telephone rings, because the caller will be no one you know. Marketers are why the sight of the mailman, which brought a smile to your face in your former country, is a dreary one here. He might as well be working for *them,* given the cheerless bundles he delivers every day. On each, tightly packed with a rubber band, the words "valued customer" are printed. Do not believe it. In the eyes of the catalogue senders, you are perfectly interchangeable with any other consumer. That is why their envelopes are addressed to you "or the current resident."

Your mailbox may be brimming with letters as time passes. Sometimes, one envelope among them will have your name in a fancy font on the front with a gold star beside it, and a line somewhere on or around that star will read, *You have been selected!* When you read "selected," you forget to ask yourself the natural questions: Why or how was I selected? All you think, your eyes fixed on the shiny seal, is that after what you have been through, your day has finally come. You are about to do as the words on the envelope instruct: "OPEN IMMEDIATELY TO CLAIM YOUR $1,000,000!!!" Be aware that you must do the opposite of what the words suggest. Do not open the envelope! Your day has not come, and if it ever does, this is not how it would announce itself.

The peculiarities do not end with the mail or the prices. The currency is stranger yet. In your former homeland, banknotes came in all kinds of colors, shapes, and sizes. A bill of a small value could never be mistaken for a larger one because it would be discernibly smaller or come in a different shade. In the mecca of capitalism, on the other hand, where choice and variety reign supreme, banknotes may as well have been designed by communists. They are uniform in both color and size. Their only variation is the portrait of the president on one side, though they, too, are all men, and mostly whiskered. Why? If the sly marketers had a say, it could well be to make the hundred-dollar bill look like the ten-dollar, so spending one in lieu of the other might happen more easily.

For the moment, American prices mean little to you unless they are converted to the currency of your past. It will take time until you adjust to the dollar and stop multiplying every price according to the daily exchange rate. Everywhere else, mathematics is about numbers and reason, except in exile. At this moment, math is only an exercise in nostalgia. The past is not past. It draws you, because it is the origin from which everything you know comes. With all that gravity still pulling at you, no wonder you have to convert the value of every product, because the values of the homeland are the only ones you trust, which is why you will continue doing the torturous multiplication for a long time to come.

When you realize the difference between what you used to pay for cereal and what you have to pay now, you gasp, toss the box back on the shelf, and curse the contents, which have obviously been individually priced! Try your best to enjoy the bounty you see without drowning in the bygone. You are here at the American feast: oh beautiful, oh smogless skies, oh infinite virtual bazaar, oh overflowing bins of seasonless fruits, oh overstocked grocery aisles, oh uncensored books in the endless electronic stores, oh newspapers and magazines of unmonitored and uninspected content . . . Think of this new life as a second one you were never supposed to have. You had only to take a plane or a boat, suffer through a difficult crossing to arrive at a place many years ahead of the one before.

THE IMMIGRANT'S TV GUIDE

Back at your apartment, the sun will still be in the sky. And you, perfectly dazed, must avoid going to bed. Television could help delay sleep. If you flip through the channels, you are bound to get to the news. You do your best to focus your attention on the broadcast. Yet the more you listen, the less you understand. You wonder what brand of English they speak, if they speak English at all. In your country, you had private tutors, attended classes at the language institute, spent hours studying. Still, you cannot make out a single word. What comes out of the correspondent's mouth are not sentences but yarns of speech that unspool with the movement of her lips. For a few moments, all you want to know is where a single line begins or ends. Is it the accent? The delivery? The speed? The camera zooms in on the close-up of the correspondent. She tips her head, pauses, smiles, and when she speaks again you hear "right back!" You cannot remember the last time you were so overjoyed at recognizing the sounds of two words.

During the commercial break, you flip through the stations again. You might see a blue monster gobbling cookies, and your heart will skip a beat. You would be surprised how comforting the sight of the familiar puppet can be. If he begins to count, you might count along with him. *This* creature you know. This English—so much more intelligible than the other—you understand. You will be overcome by a tide of affection for the monster. You had always liked him, but now he is downright eloquent and riotously funny. You might watch the entire show, something you have never done as an adult. You have yet to realize that being transplanted is a rebirth of sorts. Until you find your bearings, or master the language, you are a child again in many ways despite your size. Which is why you have a disarming effect on some native-born. Your imperfect sentences, your difficulty carrying out some of the most mundane tasks, and your vulnerable ways tug at many heartstrings. Others will assume you helpless and innocent, as long as you cannot articulate your true thoughts and feelings. Take advantage of this transient phase, where much affection and help will come your way, but it is bound to let up as you learn the proverbial ropes.

Try to watch daytime dramas. Unlike the news, the world of the soap operas is often one of slow dialogue and repetition. These two qualities will take you far in learning English. Lucky for you, the sentences spoken are often interrupted by kissing, weeping, embracing, or extreme disease, which will leave the characters either unable to speak at the speed of the news anchors or bedridden in a coma. These unusual states bring dialogues to a pause, giving you a chance to sift through the plot. Besides, the tales of excess—feverish passion, unquenchable desire, wild impulses that lead to madness, addiction, murder, and an assortment of other miseries—recur incessantly. Even if you miss them from time to time, you can always catch on, because if there is one thing you can count on to reliably happen in a soap opera it is human misconduct between the hours of twelve and three p.m. The absence of temperedness or contentedness as traits of the protagonists also gives you a glimpse of certain aspects of the American character.

Even the television will not sustain your attention after a

while, and your mind will begin to wander. You are overrun by anxious thoughts about the next day: *What will tomorrow be like?* Finding work, any work, is the first order of business. A resettlement counselor and an employment advisor are to meet you the next day. Will you be ready? Suddenly, you are too worried to lie in bed. Whenever you check the time, you think about the ones you have left behind and what they might be doing at this hour. People who are not homesick set their clocks to the standard time of their own region. But in exile, when homesickness is at a peak and every thought chases the next in a loop of regret, the hours pass according to the Standard Time of the Displaced. A minute, brimming with the urge to write a letter home or make a call, slows to an hour, and every hour is a tunnel that opens onto darkness, and leads into darkness. Here, the body may slouch toward east, west, north, or south, but the heart is ever fixed homeward, to the city you just left.

Sleep will come at last. In your dreams, your mind returns to the thoughts you had just before your eyes shut. You go home again. In that gossamer interval, you will lunch at your mother's and have tea with your best friend. An unwitting ghost, you roam through the old familiar streets until dawn. These are either where you long to be or where you most fear to be. And the morning will accordingly either strip you of the beloved visit or take you out of the hell you never want to revisit. The journey in your sleep will make you restless through the night. You went to bed with your head on the pillow, feet to the footboard. You wake up with the pillow tossed away, your feet dangling off the bed's edge, and your head in another continent.

THREE

On Résumé Writing, ESL School, and Other Post-Arrival Drudgeries

Clerks ought not to think of coming to the United States
unless they have thoroughly made up their minds to lay
down the pen and to take to the spade or the plough.

—AMERICAN SOCIAL SCIENCE ASSOCIATION,
Handbook for Immigrants to the United States (1871)

Brace yourself for job counseling. If you are a man from a chau-
vinistic culture, you will loathe the idea that both you and your
wife must attend these sessions, and other resettlement meetings, too. Worse yet, you and your wife, whom you have never
allowed to work outside of the home, must work, whatever the
job that comes along may be. The orientation class is usually
taught by female counselors—the bossy, unmarried kind you
would not want your wife to associate with.

If you are a refugee, you cannot get around these obliga-
tions. On the many forms you signed before arriving, you committed to all manner of early training and job readiness. These

were among the conditions of your admission. Day after day, you must show up at one meeting or another. You will sit in a desk chair and a woman will tower over you and ask that you repeat after her the lines she wants you to speak at a job interview. You have never followed a woman's orders, you cockily think to yourself, and you are not about to start now. You try to resist her, but not for long. She will not let you alone until you do as she asks. Scanning her from several views, you size her up and cringe that this loud, overbearing, and unappealing person should be America's idea of a woman. Who gave her permission to work? you might wonder. A moot question, because an American woman, alas, does not need permission to do as she wishes.

You sit there, listening and seething, cursing the fate that put you in that desk chair in America, where you have to follow the orders of a female who, to add insult to injury, is half your age. She insists on eye contact and then fixes you with the shameless gaze that in your tradition should always avert itself from a man. She grabs your hand to show how an American handshake is done and does not let go until she has demonstrated, skin to skin no less, all the different variations of pressure in a proper greeting, essential for a successful first meeting. This woman, who has power over so much of what happens to you for the next few months, will tell you what to wear to a job interview, make sure you shower, insist that you use mouthwash and deodorant. You wonder if there is a worse humiliation. The answer is yes, there is. If you disobey her and, say, not show for an appointment, she can cut off all your funds and other supports, and then you will have to grovel and beg her for forgiveness.

You speak to her through an interpreter. He meticulously translates everything, except for your despair. She wants you to write a résumé, which every job advertisement requires you to have. On your next visit with her, you will have to bring a first draft of your résumé. She writes the word "self-sufficient" on the whiteboard. This is what you have to become within three or, at most, six months. It does not matter if you like the work, or if you are suited for it. Attending to your hopes and plans for the future is not her concern. On the progress reports she has to turn in to her bosses, there are no boxes for empathy. You see, all bureaucracies are brainless, no matter how many oceans you cross.

YOUR LIFE ON A PAGE

However you feel about it, you must write that résumé. If you look up the word in your dictionary, this is what you will find:

> résumé *noun*
> 1
> *U.S.:* a short written description of your education, qualifications, previous jobs, and sometimes also your personal interests, that you send to an employer when you are trying to get a job:
> If you would like to be considered for the job, please submit your *résumé*.

—called also *(chiefly British) curriculum vitae*

2

formal: a short description of things that have happened: summary

The second definition is less daunting and could make it
easier for you to begin to draft the summary that would suit the
purpose. You have yet to fully grasp that while you were taking
one day at a time to cope with the crises of your old life, many
in America were enjoying all manner of personal enrichment—
attending college, apprenticing, taking on volunteer positions,
training at technical schools, studying for various licensing
exams. They took up hobbies that would make them more
appealing to their future employers—competing in sports, playing instruments, brushing up on their foreign language skills.
All the feats you performed to escape and outfox every danger,
which seemed like major triumphs at the time, warrant no mention now. There is no place on a résumé for swimming across the
Rio Grande several times to make a final safe passage, or surviv-
ing the crossing on foot despite the crooked "coyotes." You cannot brag about being the only person who survived the massacre
in your village and get no credit for successfully bribing corrupt
customs officials or perfectly forging exit documents. That was
remarkable in the other place, where everyone saw what you
saw, shed tears over the same grief, and worked as hard for the
same paltry pay. Under normal circumstances, your past is the
material of fantasies, nothing that belongs to the pages of a
résumé. You can ably walk through blistering heat for several

days without food or water? Accurately identify medicinal and other healing plants for emergency wound dressing where there is no clinic or medical professional? Stand straight-faced before guards who have detained you and lie your way to freedom? Dig deep graves with very few or no tools? Walk over a harsh terrain for long distances without rest? Learn foreign languages with no instruction, only by watching action films and listening to the BBC? Hunt, skin, and cook whatever animal when there is no food to be had? Build basic life tools—toys, kitchen utensils, cookware—from scraps and discarded material? Capably write a secret note in invisible ink—sugar water is best—to bypass the censors at the post office and elsewhere? None of these matter now, not on your American résumé.

What jobs would you list under employment? Prisoner? Peddler? Dissident? Persistent green card applicant? Those who said what does not break you makes you stronger were merely consoling you. The suffering you endured falls under no "skill," "experience," or "education." And it does not qualify you for a job. It only tells an employer the details of a past you would rather forget, let alone have others learn.

Regardless, there is no getting around writing this résumé and finding a way to summarize what you have done on an 8½- by 11-inch page, draining all its colors into simple black and white to make it all reader friendly. Leave it to America to show you how to package mayhem into something presentable. Sifting through the events, shaping the chaos in your mind, letting it all settle amid commas, colons, and periods is a good step. But it will do little for your job prospects. Still, you will place this piece of paper in a folder. You will also add to that folder the diplomas, awards, college transcripts, letters of reference from the experts in your field in your former homeland—some laminated, some fading. You had kept them so tightly close to your chest while in transit that, like some holy scroll, these pages became a part of you; every exhale came mixed with a crinkle.

You take this bundle to your next job counseling appointment, where you expect to undergo a mock interview. Before the meeting begins, you will wait in a room where a slew of people of other nationalities are waiting to do the same. None look like you, but all wear an anxious expression similar to yours. Among them are men and women, young and old, some skilled, others not. They are there to get their starts in America, and most do—they apply for a Social Security card, prepare for a driver's test, learn to fill out a job application, etc. Yet the few highly educated in the mix are the ones who best expose the flaws of the resettlement services. They are easy to spot because they distinctly set themselves apart. A husband, for instance, is likely to be in a suit, or at least a crisp collared shirt and pressed pants, his wife equally well-dressed. Though the gray at the root of the wife's blond hair betrays her age, she and he both insist on appearing younger than they are, for whatever they have yet to learn about America, they already know that it is the land of the young. The husband is clean-shaven, wearing a hint of an aftershave, which, like everything else about them, strikes the senses as foreign. The wife has bright makeup on. They may or may not have left their home that morning with a briefcase or a purse, but they will surely have a plastic bag with snacks and other essentials with them. One of them will carry a binder with original copies of the couple's university transcripts along with certified translations of each into English, and other documents—licenses, patents, letters from local officials thanking the husband or wife for exemplary performance, sample blueprints of their computer-aided designs, or book illustrations. In short, the binder is a testimony to their worth, to which their English cannot yet do justice. It holds all the supporting evidence for their high expectations from their meeting.

The resettlement counselor steps into the waiting room and carefully calls their names, say Marina and Vladimir X. They rise enthusiastically, their confidence visible in the wide grins they jointly flash at the worker. When they are seated, Vladimir reaches into the plastic bag for a small gift they have brought for the resettlement worker, usually a handmade souvenir from their homeland. He accepts the gift, holding it up to the light to admire the beautiful craftsmanship, which the husband is quick to say is the work of artisans in his birth city. He thanks them and calls the gift "gorgeous," a word that the wife, the better English speaker, does not recognize and immediately looks up on her cell phone. She does so because a serious immigrant with ambitious plans for her future will not idly nod when she does not understand something that is said. She takes matters into her own hands and treats every word as a step not to be missed toward the destination that is the American dream.

The worker places the gift on the metal file cabinet, where it joins a clutter of stapler, Post-it notes, and a few dusty photo frames. The next sound—of the binder unzipping—mixes in with the echo of "gorgeous" from Marina's cell phone. Vladimir puts an impressive pile of papers in front of the counselor. He points to one letter, sealed in gold, which bears the signature of his former state's governor, thanking him for his service as the medical chief of the largest local hospital. He offers a certified translation of the letter to the counselor, who scans it as he nods and says "Wow" a few times. "Wow" draws a second set of confident grins from the couple and the admission from Vladimir that he plans to work as a doctor in America.

Hearing this last remark, the worker's face and tone darken, and the pleasantries that had followed the gift vanish as though they were never exchanged. He shuffles through the papers to look for a copy of Vladimir's birth certificate and says, as if speaking to himself, "Let me see . . . how old are you *again?*" (Because Marina and Vladimir are not native English speakers, they do not feel the bite in the word "again," for the topic of age had not come up at all before to need revisiting. The counselor knew well how old each client was. "Again" was only an excuse to remind *them* that they are too old for grand plans.)

Vladimir says that he is forty-three. Marina, an exacting engineer by temperament and ever in charge of quality control, nods in approval. The counselor tells Vladimir that the medical equivalency exams are extremely taxing and would require Vladimir to compete against American graduates, who will be both fluent in English and nearly twenty years younger than he is. Vladimir looks to Marina and the two confer in Russian for a few moments, then he turns to the worker and, raising his index finger, he says that in his home country he placed first in his final exams. (Marina shuffles through the binder and finds a newspaper clipping with the announcement of Vladimir's great success in the nationwide tests.) The resettlement worker, unmoved, scans the clipping but does not take it from her. He reaches for a different set of papers in his own files. These are the contracts the couple had signed, promising to accept the very first job they were offered in the United States. The pair look dismissively at their own signatures and insist that they have every intention of going to work and being tax-paying citizens. In that case, the counselor tells them, he has already arranged two job interviews for them. Marina welcomes the news and wants to know more. The work, the counselor explains, is the graveyard shift in that very building, cleaning offices. "Cleaning?" a suddenly reddened Vladimir asks, his forehead knotted in a scowl. "Yes, cleaning. Nothing heavy, but yes, you know, trash cans, dusting, tidying the bathrooms, scrubbing the sinks and the bowls. The employer will tell you the details." The energetic Marina has retreated into her seat in silence. The contracts the couple had signed made no exceptions for star physicians or engineers with patents to their names. They require that all new immigrants begin earning a living immediately or within a few weeks of their arrival. Vladimir and Marina's American dreams must be dreamed some other time, some other way. Vladimir pleads to be given only a couple of months to study full-time, so that he can take the medical equivalency tests he is certain he can pass. But the counselor's responsibility is to get them jobs. What happens to the couple in ten years, or even a year from now, is not his concern. He must send them to work, any work, so that he can check a box on the "progress report" form, to show that his clients have been employed. That is the only measure of his effectiveness in the eyes of his superiors. If only the counselor had shown that he cared enough to help plan a better future for them, Marina and Vladimir would not have been so furious and brokenhearted. But he has never been a star physician or a refugee, nor does he have the wisdom to know that the people before him had not become who they were because they had listened to the officials in their own homeland. They had, indeed, succeeded in the past because they had defied every bureaucrat who stood in their way. That is what Marina and Vladimir, in the quick glance they exchanged, reminded each other of without saying a word. They storm out of the office, leaving an angry resettlement worker to find another set of graveyard-shift laborers to dust his messy file cabinet.

BACK TO SCHOOL AGAIN

To get decent work, you need to speak English, and to speak decent English, you need to be around native speakers. Since neither can wait for the other, you must somehow do both at once. So you head to the English as a second language (ESL) school. On your first visit, you will be pleasantly disappointed, disappointed because you had expected an American school not to have the same dreary institutional look, the icy fluorescent lighting and the musty smell you know so well. Pleasantly, because the fact that these are reminiscent of home is a small relief. The odor and glare make this place a little less daunting, less

American, than others you have been to so far. That you will be among dozens more who are as desolate as you will be comforting. Your real American adventure begins here, in the classroom where, for the first time, your peers are not your compatriots. Gone is the comfort uniformity offered in the past. Never before have you been among forty other people who came from dozens of countries. This is what you passingly noticed at the airport, upon reading the name tags of the customs officers. In this school, you are wading into America's ethnic soup, to mingle with so many others. You want to blend in, but your scars and scabs of past wounds need time to soften and pale, and time is what you have most abundantly. It is here that "Where are you from?" ought not to make you anxious, for it will be a genuine expression of curiosity, an invitation to friendship. When each student says the name of his or her country, you will hear of places you have never heard of before. A shoddy description of this exceptional experience of suddenly being thrust into a nation made up of so many nations is to call it a "rainbow," somehow attributing to the heavens what is, in fact, a man-made miracle. Nowhere but here do so many people live side by side in such perfectly imperfect harmony. Which is why at no time in history has a people ever been so mighty.

YOUR AMERICAN BAPTISM

After naming everyone's country of origin, the students begin to say their own names and birthdays. A surprising few share the birth date of January 1. These are a sort of born-again immigrant, for they had no birthdays when they arrived and were given the New Year's date by customs officials at their ports of entry. There are other anomalies that strike you during these introductions. The Chinese pupils who two weeks earlier had been on the streets of Shanghai introduce themselves as Jackson and Jennifer. Another, whom you know to be called Mohammad, readily sacrifices two syllables and a prophet to become merely Mo. The Scheherazade sitting beside you tells you she shape-shifted into a Sherri because her boss had wanted something simpler to call her by. She warns that if you do not choose a new name, your bosses, instructors, and others with power over you who may find your given name unwieldy will take it upon themselves to anoint you. The moral of Sherri's lesson is that from this point forward, the idea of your name, the revered family name of your father's lineage, can no longer remain solid and unchangeable. A name is like an egg now. You must learn to recognize any, every, and all its derivatives, just like the various preparations of an omelet.

When the time comes for you to introduce yourself and be greeted by others, you will gasp at hearing your name uttered by your peers. You will write it on the chalkboard, slice it up with slashes, and enunciate each syllable. Yet your beautiful name, the one your mother called you by, is downright jangled in their mouths.

Now you begin to see the foresight of Jackson, Jennifer, and Mo. Will you, too, have to give up your real name and become something foreign to yourself just to make yourself familiar to the foreigners? Will you now join the order of hopeful strangers, assume a new name, and speak in another tongue? What else and how much will you have to sacrifice at the altar of America to adjust, acclimate, and acculturate, to be in this classroom, find a job, reach your dream of becoming a faceless person in this new city? The land of liberty does not send her police to extort what she needs from you. For the price of membership, you will be tempted to surrender everything to her on your own.

There are two ways to react to this. One would be to fear that this is how America will drain you of all that you are, to replace you with whatever she has in store for you. The second, which requires a breezy disposition, would be to enjoy assuming a new name, speaking a new language, playing the part of someone you have never been. After all, a new country is a perfect stage, and seamless assimilation is nothing if not a superb performance.

TWO WAYS TO CONJUGATE

All through the lesson, an energetic teacher will pace the room, trying to ease each anxious pupil into participating. ESL teachers are often charitable, enamored of other cultures and traditions. You will be startled by how unceremoniously they enter the classroom and print their titleless names on the blackboard: Bob, Liz, Jack, Joe, Ann. They are so without pretentions and formalities that you will feel compelled to call them Mr. and Mrs. if only to lend some heft to the bare single syllable. Most of these teachers feel toward their newly arrived students as mother hens do toward their newly hatched chicks: protective, hypervigilant, ever trying to brighten the adrift and overworked immigrant's day. They resort to humor whenever possible. For instance, if a teacher plans to teach how a verb is conjugated in the present tense, he might pick one that would bring a smile to the students' faces. The laughter, he hopes, will make the lesson more memorable. Instead of using the tired "sit" or "wash," he might opt for the mildly scandalous "kiss" instead. In a two-sided chart, he will make a list of pronouns: singulars on the left, plurals on the right:

I kiss	We kiss
You kiss	You kiss
He/She/It/ kisses	They kiss

"Kiss" will have the intended effect. Giggling follows. As much of early language learning is a game of show-and-tell, the instructor will read each line and punctuate it with a smooching sound. Some of the students cover their mouths and chuckle bashfully. Others begin to banter, though in their own language. This particular laughter, rippling through the class like a warm tide, is about more than mere humor. To be in a group, and joyous, is the mark of an inclusion that to the immigrant only means that he might have, indeed, successfully made his entry, this time through another boundary, into society. It is about fitting in. It is also why whenever an immigrant fully understands a joke, the following laughter is far more raucous than warranted.

And you, emotions still raw and humorless for the foreseeable future, have slipped into reverie. While the class goes on roaring, the teacher conjugating, your melancholic mind is abiding by the grammar of yearning:

> I miss
> I miss
> I miss . . .

In the vacuum of loss, there are no second and third persons, singular or plural. For you, it will only be "miss," all pronouns vanishing but the lonely "I." Reason might make an attempt to argue against longing: *What was good about the place you left anyway?* You remind yourself of the many unpleasant things but feel no relief. It is all the imperfections of that past life that made the place you knew well and over which you had mastery. You miss loved ones, but you also miss the mastery you no longer have.

In class, your attention will eventually return. You will politely, encouragingly, listen to your classmates' attempts at proper speech, like adults listen to the cacophonous recitals of schoolchildren. A Spanish-speaking Victor introduces himself as Bictor. An Arab woman who is debuting herself as a Penelope is similarly afflicted. The Iranian in class puts an "e" before every word that starts with "s." That is how he "goes to *e*school everyday." When the time comes for the Slavs to speak, every "th" will turn into "z," their sentences resembling the static on a radio with poor reception. Betrayal comes cheaply when you are a new immigrant. A mere mispronounced letter can give away the nationality you want to hide and keep you from passing as a native.

Learning regular verbs will hearten you at first. They will make you believe that you can, someday soon, master the language. But then the irregulars will quickly humble and deflate you. It is the irregular verbs that cause you and your peers to start a small mutiny against English, and other grievances will soon follow. Someone will have a hard time reconciling with the idea that some verbs do not take an "-ed" and will insist that she "comed from." (*These* are the people who are going to become Americans? you think incredulously.) Someone else will want to know the difference between "dinner" and "supper," "house" and "home," or why anything needs to be "on top of" anything when it can simply be "above," not to mention "over" it? Another will complain that if the "k" in "knife" is silent, why have it there at all? And if the sound "-ough" is really the same as the sound "f," then why not write "enuf" instead? Nothing causes a greater debate than the enigmatic "s," which can pluralize some names, but not other names, whose logic the teacher will try to explain but without success. And for some, whose mother tongues do not have separate pronouns for the different genders, and for whom "he" and "she" are interchangeable, the two pronouns are only a source of confusion. Lastly, if English is indeed such a rich language, then why is it so poor in words describing family relations? How is it that the lexicon with hundreds of names for the various flavors of ice cream has only two words, "uncle" and "aunt," for the sibling of any parent, which does not distinguish between in-laws, maternal or paternal relatives?

The more you listen to your peers, the cockier you may feel. You are sure you can do better, speak more articulately. This class is not for you, you say to yourself; you are more advanced. English comes to you more naturally, the voice within whispers, given that your culture is richer. Then it is your turn to speak, read a passage, or repeat the words the teacher will ask you to repeat. When you do, you cannot help but feel that your classmates are snickering. The teacher interrupts you to talk about something called "emphasis." You cannot simply read what you see, he says. You must learn to place the emphasis on the right syllable. Is there a rule to know where the emphasis goes? No. Another enigma. He goes to the blackboard to explain. Certain words like "seat" have a long "e" sound, and others, like "set," have a short "e" sound. Then he asks you to repeat the two words again. You do. And once more there is snickering. When you try to read the passage he wants you to read, the words do not travel lightly from your throat to your lips. You know well what fluency sounds like, and you know that it does not sound like what you just spoke. You cannot stand hearing your own speech, especially if you care to be eloquent. You are there in the flesh and present, but the sound you make is that of a lesser, farcical thing, like a puppet in the hands of a ventriloquist. Here you might decide, highly unwisely, only to listen but not to speak until you have learned proper English.

It is a crossroads at which many immigrants arrive—at the decision whether to retreat or persist. Some prove to be turtles, others pigeons. One group retreat into themselves at the first sign of trouble. These are the people who are afraid of rejection. They sit with their pride and fester. The second group may briefly distance themselves but will return to the scene and linger for any crumb of opportunity. The latter are more likely to succeed, but no one's success is ever guaranteed. Americans like to believe that immigrants come to their country and, sooner or later, reach the "dream." This usually happens later rather than sooner, if at all. It often takes one generation or more to give its all for the next to begin to thrive. The nation's bootstraps have lately frayed, and they tear more often than help the fallen lift themselves up.

YOU, SECOND EDITION

After the first hour of ESL school, your mouth will be sore, your head throbbing. Learning to speak English is that arduous and consuming. It will feel like an hour spent climbing an unwieldly boulder. The weight of your own struggle is multiplied as you watch your classmates suffer along with you. The truth is that you would learn much more, and faster, if you could just listen to untormented English being spoken by Americans. But the company of inarticulate foreigners at the ESL school is what you can get instead. Perhaps it is a consolation to remember that this is a transient stop along the road to resettlement, one to which you will never return. This is when you and your fellow students are at your most loveable to Americans, just when you begin to learn enough to make small talk, with all the charms of one new to speech. Fortunately, you do not have the facility to speak of the bitterness you feel. Once you are more adept and can express your opinions or challenge the opinions of others, the charm will vanish and you begin to offend or peeve.

Gripped by homesickness or pressed by your own ambitions to get out of what you think of as a language ghetto, you might overlook the joys of ESL school. The struggle you experience in class as you try to learn, the humiliation you feel when you cannot express yourself, bring you close to the peers who are equally at a loss. Eventually, Christmas comes along and you have a chance to forget about English. Unburdened by language, you will all dress in your best, cook the foods you love, and let dancing do all the speaking for a few hours.

Years later, your mother tongue, so fully present to you now, will no longer be as keenly available. It will fade, like a faint sun on a foggy day. In your birth country, they are busy constructing new idioms and changing the old ways of speech. These new expressions will sound strange to you when you hear them spoken by those who arrive after you. Perhaps you will have mastered English by then, and you might even have become bilingual. When that time comes, speaking the old tongue will bring back all the feelings you had when you first arrived. If you hail from a country where there was no freedom of speech and had been raised under censorship, you will turn timid, resort to ambiguity again, use indirect and muddled language, hem and haw in response to a sensitive question. If your culture was deferential to elders, you will cast your eyes down and speak softly to your parents. You will not find it in you to challenge them or openly reject their advice. If your culture did not treat women with equal respect as men, the iciness will frost over your tone when talking to your wife, or the curtness with your children.

English, on the other hand, will liberate you, for it comes with the bold American attitude in tow. A simple switch from your language to English will have miraculous effects: You will be unchained. You will say exactly what you want and mean. You will have no qualms about objecting to your parents, or calling your wife "honey," and will address your daughter as "Her Majesty," like a dutiful subject should, as she pours you tea from her miniature tea set.

Though unimaginable now, in a few years you will accrue other incremental changes, tiny deposits into an account of belonging. You will switch from English to your mother tongue mindlessly, blending one with the other, creating what is neither exactly English nor the language of your past. It will be a third tongue, just like what you will become—a third sort of human: not the outsider that you are today, and not the undetectable insider. You will then be a twilight citizen, treading between two cultures. Your newfound worldliness will nag you at every step, like a pebble in your shoe.

FOUR

On Public Transportation, Getting Lost, and Other Post-Arrival Tribulations

The "majestic rivers," "towering mountains," "dense forests," and "fertile valleys"—so graphically described by tourists—afford the emigrant but little pleasure. Emigrating allows of no romance; there is too much matter-of-fact about it.

—MALCOLM MACLEOD,
Practical Guide for Emigrants to the United States and Canada (1870)

Time for a jaunt! On a weekend, you decide to go sightseeing. You do a bit of research and find several promising spots. Even before you set off, the addresses themselves have you smitten. Broadway, Dogwood Lane, Vista Terrace, Whispering Ivy Way . . . such ravishing names, inviting even the laziest homebody to go for a stroll. You are relieved to see that none bear the name of a martyr or remind you of any old wars and bygone enmities. Liberty, Franklin, Washington, or Independence are as political as the American block gets. You wonder if the bloody battles of the past, save a Veterans Highway, have been relegated to history books. Swan, Acacia, Falcon, and Chestnut are not the whimsical material of fairy tales alone. They adorn the cities' routes. No leader's or ayatollah's name follows the word "Grand" here. On the American street, Grand is, well, just grand. Unexceptional Mains and Broads abound. Every city will have them. The names may appear to lack heft, but they do the job of keeping the traffic going, without inflaming collective emotions. Better to breathe on a mediocre and unambitious Elm than to walk under the banner of a Valiasr, the Shiite Messiah. Better to stare into the blank distance on the bus line on Market Square than to stare at a God-sized flag of the Leader on People's Square. Better to have no more than a church bell interrupting a day's stroll than to have the muezzin blare his call five times a day. Faith, you will soon learn, is best when you turn to it at your will, not when it is peddled to you at every turn.

However, you would be foolish to think that these innocuous street names speak of an untroubled past. Freedom Lane may bring only the sunny thought of liberty to your mind. To some native-born, on the other hand, it is a reminder of the bloody struggle it took to achieve it. You believe being a newcomer—an outsider—is your disadvantage. But since you think of Washington and Jefferson as only venerable images on the banknotes in your wallet, your outsiderness becomes your advantage, too. You are not aware of the lingering torments of this nation. For you, the fully armed man on the pedestal in the middle of the neighborhood square is nothing more than a good backdrop for a selfie. For some, however, he is a ghost that still haunts them. All this is to say that you ought to delay judgment. Even after you have learned the stories that you have yet to know, you will still find something remarkable about America. You will pass through Martin Luther King Jr. Boulevard, Harriet Tubman Avenue, and Frederick Douglass Highway, and you will realize that America's mistakes are not few, but that she has the ability to correct herself, and change course.

FIRST TRANSPORTATION WOES

Until you get your own car, being carless in much of America will handicap you. Americans put a man on the Moon, but they have not done as well on Earth for public transportation. In other words, brace yourself for another disappointment. Outside of a few major cities, buses and trains will exasperate you. You walk to the bus stop, where you wait until you at last spot your bus slithering close on the horizon. From a distance, it looks as an American bus should: a behemoth advertisement on wheels, displaying images of fetching people on all sides. Stepping inside, you may be tempted to show your fare card to the driver, expecting him to collect or stamp it. You may have been used to the ritual of handing your ticket to the driver or his sidekick to rip it up. But no more! It will take several attempts for the bus driver to convince you that there will be no exchange of tickets or money and that you must simply sit. Here, as in many cities, they count on you to pay for your fare on your own.

In major cities, where the wealthy are commuters, the buses are, in fact, what you expect them to be: clean, efficient, pleasant. But in small towns, you board the bus and feel a foreboding. The faces of the bent elderly, the dozing homeless with their heads bobbing against the glass, mouths agape, and others who are clearly your alien brethren will make you realize that you are not in the land you imagined: the land of the wealthy, and of shiny, highly advanced moving machines. You understand that these sorry buses are there to, slowly and infrequently, transport the sluggish poor and vulnerable to their sorry destinations.

If you must get on the subway, you should know that more often than not, a trip down the metro's escalator, which will rarely be working both ways, takes you from the heart of the greatest global superpower into the belly of the third world. As you gape at the reeking, rat-infested, trash-strewn tunnels, you wonder if you are still in America.

In the absence of musicians playing on the platform, you may consider walking to the newsstand and scanning the magazine covers to avoid the unsightly surroundings as you wait. They, too, offer a kind of American education that you could quickly decide you would rather do without. Some of the magazines are dedicated to the celebrities and their lives—love affairs, weddings, childbirth, divorces. On the cover of one, you might see, "Hitched! Wedding Bells! Joy!" On another, you will see a slew of photos of pregnant women, or startled toddlers in the arms of a heavily disguised adult. A different cover reads, "It's War." The next: "Marriage Crumbles" "It's Over! Get Out!" "Splitsville! Downward Spiral." Under the photo of a strapping blue-eyed fellow, the caption reads, "Back on the market!" So many questions come to your mind: *Job market? Stock market? Anyhow, who would ever turn him away?* Most of these headlines fill you with dread, because they remind you, yet again, how much you do not know or understand about the new country and its people: "A Revenge Romance: Devastated Demi!" You step back to look at this from a distance to be sure you are not misreading. Still, nothing makes sense. "Khloé Pregnant! Who's the Father?" *Who is Khloé?* "The $400 Million Divorce Shocker!" The numbers are so staggering they verge on silly. "Inside Their $50 Million Mansion." There are photos of golden sinks and a glass swimming pool, the very symbols (or even less) over which nations have risen up and staged bloody rebellions. *Could there be a revolution brewing here? Will chaos follow you to America?*

A separate row displays beauty publications—on every cover, dozens of cures and advice: "Acai Berry! Eat Your Way to a New, Lighter, Younger You!" "Your Happy Fix Is Here!" Each cure is so heavily peddled that it cannot but lead to a new obsession. Then the next issue will offer new cures for the obsessions caused by the last month's featured recommendations. Only in America is the treatment for one indulgence the embrace of a second indulgence: Dear readers! Want to eliminate the smell of onion on your breath? Eat garlic!

What you find most staggering about the titles are the numbers in them. "750 Spring Looks for You!" No point is made subtly, not even when all springs last about ninety days. America's numbers outnumber all and break every scale. "623 mood boosters." This you will find instantly suspect, because you know there is no hope for any mood that needs 623 ways of boosting. Where inflated numbers are absent, hyperbole abounds: "Sexiest Man Alive!" "Sexiest Woman Alive!" There is a lot you do not know about America, and yet you cannot trust these superlatives, and wisely so. "Get Sexy: Make Him Laugh!" You ponder this and, wanting to be open and embrace this new culture, you may decide to take the advice and try to come up with a joke of your own:

Why did the chicken cross the road?
Because the farm fell into the hands of misogynists and the
coop was overrun by tyrants.
Haha?

No! Do not make any attempts at humor or try to understand it. Not for a very long time. In those early months, or possibly years, all things funny will escape you. What you will have a lot of is anger, an endless stock of it, which together with melancholy makes a humorless mix. It will take years for you to stop saying that Americans are not funny and even more years to laugh at their jokes. Many of your former abilities will be restored, some more swiftly than the rest. You will do well at work, make friends, host dinner parties. Your jokes, however, will only cause everyone to scowl. Humor will come, but only after you master culture. In the meantime, if you need to make conversation, try talking about the weather forecast. Americans can never hear enough about the weather. Its patterns and possible movements get twenty-four-hour coverage on dedicated channels. A disproportionate amount of the daily newscasts exclusively report on the various fronts crisscrossing the skies from every direction. The forecasters present all kinds of multicolored charts and graphs—a medley of arrows flashing in one corner or another—each looking ominous to your meteorologically untrained eyes. Of these, none will show what you need to know—will it rain or shine?—until after the commercial break, until you first learn of the extra creamy qualities of Jif.

In those early days, most magazine headlines will disorient you. No matter how dire the predicaments of the Demis and

Khloés may be, they can never match the dizziness of a new-comer who is thrust upon a warless world where sexy is a virtue. Sexy was probably not a compliment where you lived. Modesty would not allow such an overt reference to so private a subject. Or it could have been worse. You might be from a country where sex and sin were synonymous. Now the word that was down-right offensive a few thousand miles away is used for praise. Just as the land you have come to has little in common with where you used to be, so do the two lexicons. You will find that at times the meaning listed under a word you have looked up will do nothing to capture the connotation of a word. Dictionaries can do little to facilitate understanding when it is culture that has been upended. Many words you thought you knew will no longer mean what they once meant. Over the years, these words will transform in your mind. You will remember what you knew and thought of the word before you came, and what you know and think of the word after living in America. The jarring dis-crepancy between the two will capture not only the geographi-cal change that your journey has wrought but also the crossing your mind has had to make. The two versions of the word may be paired in your thought in the same way diet commercials pair the fat and thin before and after photos of dieters. You, too, will remember the opposing meanings—the bleak idea of the word before you arrived, the lighter one after.

When you emerge from the underground of the metro and are on the street again, prepare to get lost, and often. You might as well select a few choice expletives in advance because you will be using them. You will curse the subway, then yourself, and then the subway again. You curse once more when you realize that "Sixty-Third," though it seemed to be a straightforward destination, is not your stop. It was not the number itself you had to get right. Like the endless queue of cereal boxes on the supermarket shelves you saw on your first day, it is the special variety of Sixty-Third that matters: way, road, lane, avenue, street, court, drive, boulevard. Or the M Street you assumed was easy to find is only a hypothetical place, until you know its coordinates: northwest, northeast, southwest, southeast.

You fume. To you, this is not a simple matter of an address. It is yet another cruel reminder of your current predicament. As if your feeling like a blindfolded man walking through the dark is not bad enough, America must also play tricks to complicate everything even more. Doctors can transplant the heart of one human into another. But no one has figured out how to transplant the human himself, especially one who was chased out of his homeland. Though he looks like the rest, he is nothing like them. The experience has changed him. Fitting him back into society upon his arrival is as unnatural as training a possum to sing with the canaries. Such a malcontented person is often diagnosed with post-traumatic stress disorder. It is a term that helps everyone but the sufferer. It brands him without lessening his pain.

ARRIVAL: A TRAGEDY IN FIVE ACTS

The possum will never sing, but in case you are that malcontented immigrant, knowing that assimilation is a journey might give you some comfort. Like the stages of grief, there are also the stages of arrival: disorientation, despair, fury, acquiescence, assimilation. During the first few weeks, you will feel mostly disoriented. Your body may quickly recover from the continental change, but your mind will remain jet-lagged. A fog envelops everything you see and touch as you stagger from place to place. Despair will set in when you realize that you are at the mercy of others to get through the fog and the most mundane routines. Doubts and regrets peck at your mind, like crows at roadkill. What would have or could have been had you come here twenty years earlier? If you are young, you might think that your suffering is greater because you do not have the wisdom to know how to adapt that comes with experience. If you are middle-aged, you will think you are suffering because you have arrived too late and are too set in your ways to change. The truth is there is no good age for being uprooted, for being thrust into the belly of the unknown.

When your mind turns the doubts and the regrets long enough, then fury sets in. At times, it drowns you, as it does at moments like this one, when you find yourself lost on a strange street where you did not want to be in the first place. You cannot say how you have so much of it inside, or why or when it appears, only that it exists, and bottomlessly so. You may go to a therapist, but it might not be much help. You will first have to educate him about what you have been through, which must often include an introduction to the political history of your former country. And when you get to the personal recountings, they feel ill-suited to the serenity of the surroundings—

the soft halo emanating from the desk lamp, the fine pairing of the couch and armchair, the overstuffed bookshelves, the air whirring with the soothing sounds of the white noise machine. You may not like to be the one to dredge up the spoiled past and muddy the lovely peace of the present he has set up in that room. The therapist will avidly take notes, as if diligence alone could be a cure. He will nod or shake his head, and his expression will grow gloomier with each retelling. "You have led a hard life," he will say sympathetically. It will only anger you. *I am paying good money,* you think, *so he can tell me what I already know?* Or he may remain perfectly silent, and you will seethe even more at the thought of him having nothing to say. Besides, the caged premise of it all strikes you as insufferable: no matter where you might be in the midst of a tale, you must stop when your time is up. In between, his few responses—"How did that make you feel?"—will touch you as all American things will touch you at first: proper but unfeeling.

If your fury abates, you might get to acquiescence. One tried and trusted path to it is to think often of all the people you once knew, all those who remain behind or are still in the purgatory of transit. You would not like to lift your own mood by rejoicing in the misery of others, but facts are facts: You are better off than they are. Regardless of what you do with your life in America, having made it here is, by the standards of those still at home, an achievement in itself.

Clearly, "assimilation" is a highly charged term. For you, at this moment, it needs to be nothing more than arriving at relative contentment, finding ease in the skin of your new life.

Assimilation is not a destination. It may best be likened to a marriage. You do not have to assume all the colors of America, only know her deeply, love her despite her flaws, and live alongside her harmoniously. Unlike naturalization, assimilation has no ceremonies or certificates. Its signs are subtle: keeping up with the details of the lives of the celebrities; square dancing or attending ice-cream socials at the neighborhood church; correctly spelling words with silent consonants; having no qualms about returning an item long after purchasing it; smiling rather than cringing when you meet a uniformed official; reaching for the tissue box when you hear the national anthem; watching the Super Bowl even though you have never been able to follow the game; making a donation at the local museum on a Thursday when it is free to the public; waiting for the green pedestrian light to come on before you step onto the crosswalk on a carless road; peppering your speech with popular but frigid terms like "inappropriate"; pinning an "I Voted" sticker on your lapel on the first Tuesday in November; breezily answering when asked, "Where are you from?"; and staying up to catch a late-night comedy hour just so you can have a few good laughs before bed, because you finally get all the references. Years from now, you will be the one around any table with a gripping story to tell. You will regale the guests with the tales of your escape. You do not have to lose your accent, or change your religion, or stop practicing your traditions. Hyphens that were once mere inconveniences in English grammar are now venerated in the American culture. It is why there are so many pride parades: St. Patrick's Day, Columbus Day, Puerto Rican Day. The Italians cheer the floats of the Puerto Ricans, and the Irish queue up at the souvlaki stands at the Greek festivals. They can dance and get drunk and be merry honoring their heritage, because they are all fundamentally and irreversibly Americans.

But let us focus on the task at hand. You are out on the street and have yet to find your way to the park you set out to find. Look for a landmark to remember your location by. Make sure to choose one that is reliably immovable, like a stone monument or a major building. Do not be afraid—one day, not today—to let yourself get lost, because wonderful surprises may ensue. For an example of such serendipitous surprises by lost immigrants, see Box 1.

BOX 1

Serendipity for Two Lost Immigrants

After spending nearly a year in Europe waiting for their asylum applications to be approved, Helen and Roya X, a Jewish mother and daughter from Iran, had finally been admitted to the United States and were living in New York City. The early days were the hardest. Roya, still a teenager, was always at the edge of rage. Perfect strangers summoned it readily with their innocuous question: "Where are you from?" Each time she answered "Iran," their faces brightened and they said that she was lucky to be out of there and in America. That she, driven from her homeland, did not wish to be in their presumed paradise never occurred to them.

What anger strangers didn't summon in Roya, her relatives did. Those who had come years earlier assumed themselves authorities on all matters. First there was the barrage of metaphors to set the mother and daughter on the right track: "You're a bird now. You migrated to where the weather is better." Or "You're a plant and this is good earth for your roots at last." Being perfectly disoriented, Roya and her mother believed that if only they dressed their minds in the right metaphor, their dizziness would end. In the new country, they knew they had to begin anew. To make themselves do so, for a while the daughter invented her own metaphor. Not a beautiful metaphor, but a practical one. She imagined herself a secondhand car whose odometer had been reset to zero by exile. With all the old parts, she was recast as a brand-new human engine. Within her was all the clanking, hissing, and racket of past rides, but she had to learn to muffle them and press on.

There was also a slew of unsolicited advice, mostly contradictory, that the relatives dispensed to them. Some insisted, "Mind your own business!" Others said, "Unless you know everyone's business, you'll never get ahead." But they were unanimous about one thing: "Beware of the blacks!"

The mother and daughter had been together day and night since they arrived a few weeks earlier. Then on a blistering December day, the two had gone to Manhattan, but could not return home together. Roya had to stay for a job interview, and her mother needed to rush home to prepare the family's first Hanukkah dinner in the new country. Roya, who could speak some English, walked her mother to the subway station. Speaking like the mother to her mother, opening and closing the fingers of one hand in the mother's face, Roya kept repeating, "Remember, Mother! Fifty-Fifth Street is your stop." Then came the announcement: "Stand clear of the closing doors!" The words, tinny and unfeeling, blared through the station and did what nineteen years had not done. The two parted from each other at last.

As her train took off, Helen waved and tried to smile reassuringly. Roya flashed the fingers of her hand, mouthing the word "five." She could not be sure if she had done the right thing to let her go on her own. Just at that moment, a voice on the intercom announced, "This B train is now running on the R line. Attention: The Brooklyn-bound B will be on the R Queens line." Standing on the platform, knowing that her mother was on the wrong train, she knew then they were neither birds nor plants, for neither would ever be as lost as her mother was at that moment.

Roya took the next train home. At the local police station, she stopped to report her mother missing but was told nothing would be done until forty-eight hours had passed. So she rushed home to call their relatives. The family's first holiday in America was on the verge of becoming a disaster. The sun had nearly set and she was about to leave home to look for her mother when the doorbell rang. There at the threshold, Helen stood jubilant, her arm looped around the arm of an African American woman in a Metropolitan Transportation Authority uniform. When Helen stepped into the house, tears began rolling down her cheeks.

Following the stream of tears came the story. After more than an hour, she was the only one still on the train. Then turning her wet face to her companion, she said in Persian, "This woman, right here, saved me!" "Hey, I was just doing my job!" said the woman, surmising Helen's meaning through the tears. Then she told Roya that seeing how anxious her mother was and how little English she spoke, she thought it was best to bring her home after her shift had ended.

That night in their living room, Helen lit the Hanukkah candles, shut her

eyes, and prayed for the safety and well-being of Gloria, her newfound friend,
and all her family. She did not let poor Gloria go home to tend to her baked ham,
for Christmas coincided with Hanukkah that year, until she had tried Helen's
tarragon meatballs first.

Watching Gloria try her mother's cooking, and ooh and aah with every
bite, Roya realized that as new immigrants, they were not birds or plants but,
indeed, used cars, here to discover the vast new American road without anyone's
instructions, all on their own.

VIVA LA LIFE! DOWN WITH DEATH!

If you come to a pristine ground where juniper trees, azalea bushes, and manicured lawns are enclosed in wrought-iron fences resembling the parks you remember, do not assume they are the same. Before you spread a blanket and start your picnic, check to see if there are stone slabs dotting the ground. American cemeteries, sometimes vast and majestic, are right inside cities, next to the pharmacy, schoolyard, or gas station. Unlike the burial grounds you might have known—the gloomy over-crowded expanses outside the city limits—the dead here are mostly kept within metropolises. Americans do not fear their deceased or try to hide or avoid them. Several of their earliest cemeteries were, in fact, meant to be used as parks by visitors. Of these, some still continue to attract visitors, who also often volunteer to keep the grounds tidy, tend to the flowerbeds, and clean the gravestones of strangers. This nation has no trouble passing by their dead as they go about the business of life. The departed remain among them, their resting places a natural part of cityscapes.

Just as the dead do not stop the living, neither does death

itself. Americans mourn differently from most. Grief slows them only briefly. The weight of it will bear on them, but as they love life, they will not let it break them, not even at times of great disasters. "Move on" is a popular catchphrase here. Some even turn their grief into another reason to live, a new crusade against what caused that death to sustain them through their dark hours. Then again, with the boundless, God-given and man-made choices that are on offer, life in America is far more alluring than in most other places. "Move on" is easier to do here, where the waters are endless, the landscape is vast, and the wars are waged elsewhere.

Americans move on, and so does their calendar. Or perhaps they move on because of their calendar. The American calendar is designed to remind the citizenry that they are expected to be joyous. Amid the freeze of December over much of the nation, Christmas comes along. Weeks in advance, stores offer sales to draw people in. Dreary streets, bejeweled by lights, shed the grayness of winter. Whatever your faith, you will find it hard to resist the lustrous charm of the Christmas tree and the ribboned mysteries beneath it. Iced-over front yards warm under the glow of the nativity scene, Rudolph, and Santa. With its boundless ornamental flourishes—the numerous horned, corpulent, or diminutive creatures in its narrative—and the stream of films that are released for the occasion, Christmas is the best-produced holiday anywhere.

Then along comes January with Martin Luther King Jr.'s birthday. Note the word "birthday" as opposed to "death day." Americans could have chosen to mark the dramatic day of

Dr. King's assassination. Somber crowds would have had every reason to march on the streets and shed tears over his martyrdom. Instead, they celebrate his birth. Schoolchildren put on their best to sing songs at their assemblies and remember his legacy. Everyone professes to "have a dream" on the third Monday in January, even those who may prefer to forget the man and his cause. In the battle between joy or gloom, you can always count on Americans to choose the former.

There is Valentine's Day, with its diamond rings, flaming hearts, and mounds of chocolate. There are pride parades, Halloween parades (though the skulls and ghoulish hands planted in the gardens have yet to bring a smile to your face), Mardi Gras—none a lugubrious affair. Small communities hold local contests of pie baking, hot dog eating, pumpkin growing. There are beauty pageants, car and horse races, golf and tennis tournaments, marathons, biathlons, triathlons, and all sorts of other competitions. There are still smaller events that will not make the calendar: ice-cream socials, bake sales, Rotary and book clubs, library and community center readings, scouting events, bingo and prom nights, school plays and graduations. Even at Easter, it is not the specter of the martyred prophet—his bloody ankles and thorn-pierced brow—that is in shop windows or on front doors, but that of hopping bunnies and straw baskets brimming with colorful eggs. Americans have an uncanny ability to plan and organize for the future, invent reasons to look forward to another day.

But the occasions of America's worst defeats are kept in the history books. The calendar only notes the victories, like on July 4. The sound of fireworks will rattle you and the smoke will remind you of the unhappy fires of the past, and yet even you recognize this to be a cheerful affair. All the soldiers who have fallen will be celebrated at once on Veterans Day, and with much pomp and circumstance. As with every American holiday, stores will have major sales. Buying things in America is a patriotic act. Others lost their lives so, among other privileges, the nation can shop. Even the anniversary of 9/11, a day that more than any other deserves to be called a national day of mourning, is instead called the National Day of Service and Remembrance. Why grieve when you can perform an act, however small, to better the country?

Then there is Thanksgiving. While you might have been hesitant about Christmas or Easter or not gotten accustomed to the smoke and racket of the Fourth of July, you will find Thanksgiving and its trappings—the sacrificial bird, the bland side dishes—easy to embrace. It is the only holiday that you are confident you can improve upon. You will accept the bird as a compromise, then fuse every dish with the elements of your own cuisine. Whatever else you may not yet know, you are already certain that this young nation needs to learn a thing or two about food, for it treats herbs as disposable garnish and places salt above all other spices.

Your calendar was different. It may have been a lunar one with months and a new year of its own, in which case it will take a long time for your post-arrival dizziness to abate. Most of the observances on your calendar were mystical, or religious, or commemorated the dead. Or they marked past losses or victories—little to celebrate for the sake of being joyous without grave historical excuses weighing on everyone. Old remembrances crowded your calendar because the future was grim and uncertain. Your holidays honored a god or several of them or the celestial bodies. There were no shortages of saints, prophets, deities, and beautiful myths. Most of them took your mind off life here on Earth and turned your attention to the invisible and the immaterial. In America, on the other hand, whimsy is the stuff of the arts and films. The events on the calendar are to boost communities and give everyone a reason to be festive.

If you are from a nation ruled by a theocracy, your calendar was likely overflowing with somber events like the deaths of various prophets and saints. Large-scale happiness is a production that requires tools—music, dancing, drinking, flamboyant displays—that are usually banned under religious rule. Food, therefore, not only filled the stomachs but made up for the absence of all that could not be had. Perhaps you come from a land steeped in instability, where chaos has made routines obsolete and time is punctuated mostly by crises. Under such circumstances, every celebration—say a wedding in a war-torn city—becomes, more than anything, an act of resistance, which is not to be confused with revelry. Under war or tyranny, you did laugh, told jokes, went to parties. You defiantly danced, worrying whether the bombs might fall or the morality police were going to barge in. And joy, that easy feeling of lightness, was lost to you. Now, you have to learn it for the first time, or all over again. It will not come easily, but it will come. Some cataclysms, like the ones you may have known, change the landscape of a soul.

OF HEAVEN AND HELL IN THE AMERICAN PARK

At long last, you will arrive at your park. A park is where you have always gone to stroll, people watch, and breathe fresh air. Here is where you will take your first snapshot to send home. Your instinct is to stand against the most eye-catching backdrop, to impress friends and family with the grandest views of America you can find. But these parks fall short of your expectations. The truth is you have known better parks, and so you decide to wait for a more striking view.

You will spot the familiar water fountain but wonder if it is safe enough to drink from. Yes, go ahead! American pipes deserve your trust. And yet, many pedestrians stroll past with fashionable water bottles with ergonomically designed spouts and an added twist of herbs and vitamins to bolster health and the manufacturer's price. If you happen to be at the park on a mild sunny day, you will see much that resembles what you expect. You will find perfectly trimmed shrubs, orderly flower gardens, a fountain or two inside a majestic pool with water-spouting lions and other stony creatures beneath its shower. There will be benches under the pleasant shade of old trees, playgrounds with children swinging on the swings or sliding down the slides, tables with the elderly hunched over them, some playing board games.

But unlike the parks you are used to, you will also see runners speeding past, oblivious to everything but the music in their ears—men with inflamed cheeks, their foreheads wet with sweat; women with their ponytails bobbing to each footfall. Running was what you did when you had no choice, because you were being chased by gangs or agents of the intelligence ministry. Here, not only is running a leisure act, but people pay to hang off bridges and jump out of airplanes. It will amaze you to see tents propped up in the woods and campers struggling to start a fire. You will soon learn that people living in homes with electricity and running water, who were not forced to flee these comforts, develop a hankering for occasional self-inflicted inconvenience, such as sleeping in the bug-riddled outdoors and no outhouses. What you knew to be conditions of distress are astonishingly a sort of sport, a way to spice up the calm course of daily life in America.

Far more terrifying than the bungee jumpers are two men, arms looped in each other's arms, hands tucked in each other's back pockets. You knew two kinds of gay men in your country. The gay men among the powerful, whom everyone knew were gay but dared not call them so, and were, therefore, always safe in the silence granted to them. Then there were ordinary gay men, who were harassed and treated violently by average citizens and the authorities alike. That is why seeing the two men walking together scares you, until you remember that you are here, in the land of whatever you wish to do goes, as long as you do not harm anyone while at it.

In the distance where the park's main plaza is, hundreds of people have gathered, their sounds drowned by muffled banging and distant clatter. You flinch. Large crowds have always meant a demonstration and riot police in your memory. You remember tear gas and sirens. You inch closer to the crowd. Then you see men and women, old and young, some sitting on blankets and chairs with picnic baskets, some standing and swaying, others holding one another. A musical band on a makeshift stage comes into view, testing their instruments. Yes, music under the sky, and no arrests. It is possible.

You cannot stomach large crowds yet. They still summon the old fears in you. You walk toward the more secluded parts of the park. Your eyes will rove about but pause at a middle-aged man in only a pair of shorts lying on the grass—one hand holding a beer can, the other rhythmically slapping his hairy paunch as he tosses his head from side to side, muttering a song to himself. Half clad and fully unappealing, perfectly lost in his own world, he basks in the sun. Others walk by paying him no heed. When you were in your autocratic homeland, dreaming your grand dreams of freedom, he was not the image that came to mind. Then, freedom was a majestic thought. You could not exercise it but secretly worshipped it. In its abstract and unimplemented form, freedom was a sacred and innocent thing, painted on the walls of official buildings as a soaring bird. Freedom was the material of anthems, whose mention was followed by drums and marching bands. When you were thinking, reading, writing pamphlets about liberty, clandestinely distributing them at night, you had not thought of its routine, humdrum manifestations in the lives of ordinary people, such as the homely man before you. He is no bird. But lying there undisturbed in his happy stupor, dressed as he likes, he represents the real look of freedom far better than any avian.

You might also see a woman who is gazing at the baby suckling at her breast. For a moment, you are curious to know if you can see the breast, but admonishing yourself, you quickly look away. You never thought that in the heart of America, where privacy is a well-guarded right and innovation an article of national pride, you would catch a mother in so primitive an act and in public no less, like the poor village women you once knew.

You scan your surroundings again. Not far from the shirtless man, a young couple lie together. The woman is lithely pecking at the face of the man beneath her. Scandalous, you think, but you cannot look away. She lowers herself playfully, steals a kiss, then moves her head to the side of his face to whisper in his ear. He laughs. Her long golden hair, cascading down to his face, glints in the sun. He brushes her hair back before she lowers her face onto his again. Another kiss! This one lasts longer. They seem blissful and serene. You, on the other hand, are the one with the racing heart. He clasps his hands around her back, scoops her, and in one swift toss, he lies on top of her. She lets out a scream, then a laugh. You had seen many things in a park, on the grass, under the sun, but not this. This brazen display is indeed sex, or the most you might have ever seen of it in public.

Whether because your culture demanded modesty or religious edict outlawed any contact between the sexes, physical expressions of love were unseen where you grew up, which is, in part, why you cannot but gawk. This animal play, with no sign of fear or regard for anyone around, is not the love you knew. The warnings you had once heard begin to echo in your head, reminding you of the evils of lust. But when you gaze at the couple before you, what comes to mind is joy, beauty, desire, not evil. How can it corrupt anyone, if the passersby—those supposedly at risk—pay no heed and are simply busy jogging, nursing, drinking, and playing their board games? It is too early to acknowledge that you have been duped, that living ascetically as you did for so long simply stripped you of so much pleasure.

Still, the scene has unleashed a small mutiny within you. You want to know what it is like to scoop another, especially out in the open, or to be the one scooped. The couple's love play seems so second nature to everyone in the park but you. To them, the pair is like another shirtless man or breastfeeding mom. Like your sense of freedom, your notion of coexistence was hollow. Your idea of it was far too dreamy, not resembling its reality at work before your eyes. And this medley of human presence all under the same sun, on the same grass, each at peace with the other, is how democracy manifests itself on an ordinary Sunday afternoon.

Suddenly it will occur to you that this, in fact, is the best backdrop for the photo you wish to send home. Against the distant image of the lustful pair and the semi-naked others around, you in the foreground will seem to have arrived in more ways than one. Besides, you want a picture to remember the first time you saw a couple entangled in love in broad daylight. So much of your life had been defined by the preoccupation with less than what you see before you—dreaming of a kiss, an embrace, an arm-in-arm stroll in the park, or even an hour of undisturbedly sitting beside a lover, talking without fear. Sins are clearly harder to come by here. In America, God presides over weightier matters than the minutiae of mortals' liaisons and romances. In this park, vice abounds, but there are no fines or punishments; no lashes, no morality police, and no Satan! Only a few signs of sunburn, but no hellfire. What a difference a few thousand miles make.

PART II

FIVE

Welcome to Selfistan

It is as if the experience of being in love could only be one
of two things: a superhuman ecstasy, the way of reaching
heaven on earth and in pairs; or a psychopathic condition
to be treated by specialists.

—RAOUL DE ROUSSY DE SALES,
"LOVE IN AMERICA," *The Atlantic,* MAY 1938

Any serious talk about Americans' idea of love, their relationship to their body and sexuality must, oddly enough, begin with
a talk about democracy. The mention of the word usually brings
the ballot box to mind. But the blissful and the unaware who
are born and raised in the United States are heirs to the immea-
surable boons of this unsentimental gift, which seemingly has
no relevance to the matters of the heart. To put it simply, the
fortunate native-born are unlikely to see that the footsteps of
their founders do not stop at Capitol Hill but reach into their
most private spaces, even as far as their bedrooms. All American relationships, whether between two lovers, or government
and citizen, or mother and son, are influenced by the funda-

mental American ideas that are in the country's makeup. Just as the American land is blessed with endless waters and woods all around, the American himself and his most basic interactions are blessed by the original guiding principles that have shaped this society and are as ingrained, and thereby as implicit, as the landscapes of beaches and the forests that abound.

In the gym, for instance, where the fitness enthusiast lifts dumbbells, he is exercising both sinew and self. In courtships, the virtues of the former need no elaboration. Those of the latter, which are arguably even more instrumental, are less known. There he goes for an hour or two, with the intention to do nothing but tend to himself. The sinew he can see bulging in the mirror; the self swells within. Two forces drove him there, but he is aware of only one—his own resolve. The other is a tradition that has insisted on his singular importance as a person and raises the common individual to the same standing as the nobility. So he believes that he has inherent value, which is how the uniquely American idea of "taking care of oneself" is born. One must always guard one's valuables. In America, that treasure is, above all, the self. And it is the treasured and ministered self that makes a proper paramour.

THE BIRDS, THE FISH, THE TREES, AND THE FOUNDING FATHERS

Just as the American has inherited the color of his eyes from his forefathers, so has he inherited the belief that he is entitled to life, liberty, and the pursuit of happiness from the Found-

ing Fathers. This pursuit tethers him to the material world. He
knows life is transient. He might even be a believer and think
that there is another world to come. But while here, he intends
to stay as long as possible. To live fully in the physical world requires that he live and know fully the physical body—the chief
instrument for navigating that world. How else could he possibly get to liberty or happiness if he does not first pay life its
utmost due? Not the metaphysical life, but the real one in all its
many earthly details. Americans have a god, but their god does
not stand in the way of loving the material world. He does not
tell them to forgo joy or success and is not impatient for them
to leave the Earth. It is easier to build a future when that highest authority approves your agenda.

Every spring, wildlife societies hold special programs. Bird
lovers gather in the early hours of the day—binoculars dangling from their necks, guidebooks in their hands—to tiptoe
through the woods and catch a glimpse of, not simply birds,
but highly specific birds with multipart names, like a yellow-
bellied sapsucker. Then a dozen adults stand motionless, sup-
pressing their sneezes and coughs for many minutes to watch
a cardinal flap its wings or a yellow-rumped warbler give out
its call. They establish societies for the enthusiasts wishing to
celebrate and preserve these creatures. They photograph the
bird and mull over its beak, claws, wingspan, or the colors of
the male feathers as opposed to the female, then they record
its call and hold meetings to collectively contemplate their
observations. The trees they come upon during their walks have
plaques, their names inscribed upon each, along with their sci-

entific titles and other qualities. In the displays of their aquariums, there are boundless fish—some large and fearsome, others barely visible—each with its own name and elaborate description. In short, if it bobs, breathes, or blossoms, Americans will study it, anoint it, photograph it, preserve it in a glass case, and write books about it. Observing such objects or creatures—mammoth or minuscule—further bonds them to the physical world. When you meet groups of passionate birdwatchers, you will laugh at them at first, because you think these activities silly and frivolous. But in time, as you learn to live without fear, your mind will get roomier, your spirit more generous. Your curiosity will grow. You might even look up yellow-bellied sapsucker in the dictionary to see its image and find what it is called in your mother tongue. If you do look it up, you will most likely see either no equivalent or only the scientific name, which will be in Latin but not in your mother tongue. Then you might consider buying binoculars of your own. And why is this all possible in a democratic society? Because large swaths of time and space open up in the lives of those who no longer have to stand in line for basic daily staples or be anxious about the conflicts and crises that authoritarian governments invent to keep the masses busy.

Because achieving happiness is a national ambition, the gym-goer is determined to find it. He will not postpone bliss to some future in another dimension. He seeks it as best as he can here on Earth. Tyrannies urge their citizens to loosen their ties to the material world. They want them ready to sacrifice themselves for a higher cause, become martyrs. Some even promise paradise with all manner of heavenly perks. To be ready for that moment of sacrifice, the citizen surrenders his attachments—to loved ones and other earthly belongings, among them his own body. For Americans, heaven and all its promises can wait. They are in no rush to part with life, which is why their vitamin and supplement industry is a booming business.

To lead his life safely among others, the American, i.e., the gym-goer, does not have to belong to a tribe, an ideology, or a religion to be deserving of a bright future. Nor is it guaranteed that he will reach it, but he expects it to be his, as long as he does his part—plays by the rules and works hard. As this democracy is far from perfect, the laws do not always work as they should, and sometimes the gym-goer may fail despite his best efforts. But knowing that such a promise is there gives him confidence. America is, more or less, designed to help him. He is the one around whom this universe turns. He is not part of the hordes, as in the believers, masses, proletariat, downtrodden, tribesmen, brothers and sisters. In theory, no one can deny him a place at the proverbial table because he is the color or the creed that he is, though when it comes to the nonwhite race, the promise has not fully turned into reality.

Leaves of Grass may take his imagination only as far as the lawn of his backyard. Yet, as he pumps iron, watches his every movement, perfects his physique to his own liking, he is Whitman's progeny: *He exists as he is, that is enough.* His highly positioned ancestors devised a way to perpetually have his back. They insisted on his personhood in so many ways. This has always been a tenet of American conviction, passed down from the highest authorities. President Woodrow Wilson put it best when he said, "A man who thinks of himself as belonging to a particular national group in America has not yet become an American." Anyone from such distinguished paternity *should* gaze at himself, because he is the lucky one, the American one. And he counts.

THE AMERICAN: A TRIBE OF ONE

He counted from the start. His parents were proud of him long before he had done anything remarkable. If he only slid down the slide, they exclaimed, "Good job!" as if he had conquered gravity. If he walked without wobbling or finished his plate of food, they boasted of him. Pride did not have to be earned. It was his for simply being *him*. In kindergarten, a day would come when he would have to dress in his best outfit, comb his hair, and put on his brightest smile for the photographer. On a page, in a book full of his classmates' photos, a square space would be his, where his portrait would appear above his name in bold black print. At the age of six, even before he could read fluently, he loved to find his face in the sea of faces and look at his name in print. Every new school year, his presence was recorded with a new photo in a new book. Every American child will have his name committed to print in this way. Most lives in the world come and go without a trace, but the American student will be remembered, in twelve volumes, a small library by any measure, for no reason other than having showed up at school. He had always known he was there to learn to read and write, make maroon lava bubble out of a handmade volcano, or stand onstage, stare blankly into the dark, and enunciate, "To be or not to be." What he did not know was that he was also learning to shape a self. There was never a guarantee that he would achieve this, and anyway, it is not all that clear what it takes to make a self, or what it means to be an individual. But at the core of the American spirit is the quest to seek that self, then define it, and blare it to everyone. That is why the American bumper is overloaded with stickers, and the American skin with tattoos.

You, on the other hand, did not have a yearbook, or proms for that matter. The culture that always insisted on keeping the individual in a proper, governmentally manageable size did not care about fostering the fledgling feelings of the nation's children. You went to school to learn to worship, memorize, serve in the bondage of homework, and brood over whom to dodge and how, and if another life could be possible. You were rarely in a laboratory or working hands-on at any project. There were few field trips. Instead of dissecting cadavers, you looked at them in fading print and poor-quality photos. You had fat textbooks and practiced endlessly for tests but rarely read or even had access to any outside reading that the ministry of education had not approved. School did not aim to make a reader out of you, but a studier and memorizer of what was handed to you from above. That is why your schools had no libraries. You were never asked to offer an opinion about the topic at hand. The most serious learning you could do was to lock yourself in a room for days on end to cram for an exam. Most people around you accepted this fate. But something in you would not surrender to what most others did. All the rising or the setting of the sun began and ended with the flick of the light switch in your study. You became a ghost in your own home, pale and irrelevant to all that went on around you. A high score was your single obsession. You did not aim to become a scholar or deepen your knowledge of any field in particular. You aimed at becoming a master test taker. When you left your country on a student visa to study in America, even *you* did not realize that you were an educational refugee, a person who had never experienced the thrills of open discussion and free inquiry.

In your birth country, the family is the unit of the community. The destiny of everyone in the family is a collective destiny, their successes and failures shared among all. In America, the individual is the unit. Parents encourage their children to part from them at a young age. Some Americans send their seven-year-olds to summer camp for weeks on end, and most demand that their children leave home at the end of high school. Even if the children have not married, the American custom requires that they move out, live alone, and take their own chances at life. Nowadays, more and more American youths cannot afford to leave home. But it is what they wish to do, what some of their early success is measured by.

Your culture, on the other hand, praised togetherness, modesty, and hard work. The less you demanded, the better a pupil, a citizen you were. The moral of many of your childhood tales was to work hard, suffer in silence, and wait to be acknowledged someday, by God, or a boss, or a superior. Success in your culture was to blend into the crowd and do your best in perfect anonymity. There was no reason to think of a self. While you were leading your indistinct existence, a good many of your American peers were contemplating their innermost selves in their therapists' offices.

WHERE "I" IS KING

You should learn sooner rather than later that "you" and "I" are America's most celebrated pronouns. "He," "she," "it," "we," or "they" cannot begin to compete. In fact, "you" and "I" are among the most frequently used words in the English language. Schoolchildren are taught to avoid vague usages like the passive voice, or sentences whose subjects are obscure. However clumsily, they learn to boldly begin with "I" and forcefully state what the "I" sees, hears, feels, and believes in. "I" might loathe the pressure of this, or have nothing printworthy to report, but will eventually come to speak directly, however poorly, learn to articulate his hopes and expectations, even if insignificant.

You, on the other hand, had to dodge the censors and other bureaucrats all your life. You worked hard to master the art of disguise, hiding your feelings and intentions. This had been such a long-standing exercise in your culture that ambiguity, your most effective tool against inquisitive officials, became a mark of wisdom and, in time, a standard of literary beauty. The English style and its famous tenets—simple, direct, concise—in your former language would only lead to arrest, interrogation, and imprisonment. Even if the censors were not a concern, you would be thought immodest if you used too many "I's" in your prose. Directness was unseemly. It was the equivalent of staring someone in the eye, a disrespectful thing to do. So the "I" paled in the text, and elsewhere, too. The paling suited the purposes of the political powers well. After all, a nation of selfless people is easier to subdue than a nation made up of entitled selves.

Americans lead with "I." Lean in, they recommend, in praise of self-assertion. You learned not to be overt about your wishes and leave them for the reader to glean and interpret. But in American prose or conversation, vagueness has no place. It will only cost you dearly here. You must learn to say what you want, not shyly stand by and pray that others might be charmed by your demure hints at it. No one will dislike you for asking for what you want, but they may well find your hints mystifying and think you inept for not speaking up.

The "I," however brazen and sometimes shrill, has enriched America in so many ways. Their poetry, a case in point: It is only a few hundred years old, while yours might date back a millennium or more. Yet, whereas your nation has a more ancient poetic tradition, American poetry surpasses, in themes and fullness of expression, all the poetry in your literature. The boons of democracy are never-ending, where the unfettered artist, with his brawny self, can speak, write, paint, and do what his imagination may conjure. God, death, king, country, nature but mostly as proof of God, certain permissible kinds of love with its literary by-products—longing for the distant lover, unrequited affection, the impossibility of attaining the beloved—all existed in the poetry of your homeland. But there was hardly ever a line about the suffering of a wife at the hands of her abusive husband, the desire of a man to live with another man, the torment of a child who has been molested, or the desolation of a patient in a psych ward. In your culture, poetry was deeply esteemed. At funerals and celebrations, reciting a poem was a ritual. Guests at dinner parties entertained their host with poetry, each trying to outdo the other by reciting the longest poem by heart. There was no absence of love or regard for the art, only an absence of freedom, which muddied expression and bounded the imagination.

You wonder how this knowledge of the "I" and its footprint in English prose is of any use to you at your newly arrived stage. To begin with, if you plan to enroll in college, you should postpone taking Writing 101, or if you must, you should take it pass/fail. However good a writer you were before, you will not shine here, not soon anyway. Learning to write in English for American readers is not only a matter of translating your meaning from one tongue to another, but of peeling away at yourself and learning to think and speak in ways that you never have before. You may be required to do precisely the things you were told not to do, and not do precisely the things you were told to do. You will have to unveil your intentions and present your ideas in the most direct fashion possible. But before your sentences can rise to such occasion on the page, you must learn to do so yourself, inside your own head.

THE EXCEPTION OF THE AMERICAN FAREWELL

In this kingdom of "I," there are small signs in the mundane routines to remind you of the cultural priorities. The popular sign-off, for instance, is "Take care of yourself!" In most other parts of the world, farewells are metaphysical wishes. The departing person is left to the care of God or some mystical power. Americans, on the other hand, will not resort to the heavens, spirits, ancestors, or anything ambiguous or impractical. They do not leave the departing person in the hands of an invisible deliverer. No "May God be with you" here. The idea of "me time" is so quintessentially American that it might as well be dressed in a Stetson and a pair of cowboy boots. The advice of the how-to books, talk show hosts, and their doctor sidekicks all hammer this home. It is not only the gym-goer who has taken this to heart. Even the melancholics who spend much of the day on the couch believe this and despair because they cannot do for themselves what they are told they should.

You will not truly understand, at least not right away, that in America the first and foremost person to be cared for by you is you. Hearing the command to "take care of yourself" in those early days will startle you. Is it a warning? you wonder, and immediately worry what the concern might be that would require you to exercise care. You may even take it as a disguised threat and be tempted to say in return, "I'm good right here, sir! You watch your own back!" Eventually, you will see that there need not be any danger looming for you to look after yourself, for the self is at the center of American attention.

"Take care of yourself" conveys so much more of this nation's spirit than all the lessons you will learn in acculturation classes. There they will give you the Declaration of Independence to prepare you for the civics and citizenship exam, but no one will ask you to look for the traces of Paine and Jefferson in the routines of American life today. You will be stunned by how the grouping of a few ordinary words can create such an extraordinary text. You wonder if the native-born truly grasp that the pairing of "unalienable" and "rights" is an invention as groundbreaking as that of the steam engine. You have never forgotten that in your birth country, most rights were the occasional privileges of a few. You are tempted to ask the civics instructor if he is aware that there is nothing "self-evident" about the notion of all men having been "created equal." The matter of Earth's flatness had long been settled by the time the Founding Fathers came along. Their astronomical ingenuity was to begin to make the possibilities on the American earth flat for all. If only their "all" had not been limited to men of the same complexion, they might have been worshipped today as the Founding Gods.

You will do well to ponder these documents. Resettlement workers and job counselors will help you learn the traffic rules and you will eventually drive. But how will you find your way in the society, make sense of its demands and codes? The documents will help your social navigation. Not the native-born, who have no other reference, but only you, who has lived without their privileges, can see how these rights have gone from the page to breathe among the people. Only you, whose ambitions had always to be tamed, by the fear of God, elders, or the Leader, can recognize the majesty of the American design.

NOW IS THE AMERICAN FUTURE

The grand design, which tightly ties American citizens to the material world, cultivates a mighty enthusiasm for the future, to which the pursuit of happiness will lead. Walk into a shoe store in August to purchase a pair of beach sandals and you will only find a few odd-sized ones left. Instead, the stock of waterproof boots for winter will be overflowing. Stop at a clothing store in February for a woolen scarf and bikinis will be on display. Americans say that they "look forward" to the future. But in truth, they pounce on the future like beasts on their prey.

This fervor for the future has turned Americans into a nation of avid planners. They make all kinds of calculations from birth. Grandparents and parents start savings accounts and education funds for the newborn in their families. College students meet with job recruiters. New graduates talk to retirement advisors. Brides book ballrooms years in advance. Party planners send "Save the Date" cards months ahead. They even plan where the invitees will sit. Their names are printed on cards with numbers assigned to them, lest someone sit beside another without prior design. Pregnant mothers with means look into daycares and waitlist their unborn babies for kindergarten. In the midst of January, parents register their kids for camp in July. Families buy airline tickets for their vacations long before they mean to travel, then purchase books and study guides and watch movies to eliminate the chance of encountering anything unanticipated. Whatever Americans may or may not be, this much is certain: they are planners. Impromptu in America is mostly a musical term, not a life exercise.

An injury devastates them, but often they will rise to turn the loss on its head. A man with a missing leg will train for a marathon, a woman who survives cancer goes on to start a support group for others going through the same experience. In every anomaly, the American sees an opportunity to create something original. For the American, there is always too much to do, too much to see, too much to anticipate to wallow in grief or the thought of death. When the two planes struck the towers of the World Trade Center on 9/11, New York City appeared as it never had. The skyline smoldered. A gray rain of ash fell for days. The sidewalks that usually teemed with passersby were deserted. The blare of sirens drowned all other sounds. In the city of mischief and abandon, armed guards mushroomed at intersections, tunnel entrances, the foot of every bridge. The city that never slept slipped into a coma. Yet, despite all the threats that followed, New York began breathing again within days. Seeing her return to life was as astonishing as the attacks themselves. The buildings that had been damaged or collapsed remained closed. The rest were quickly abuzz once more.

When tragedy of such magnitude strikes, you might discover things you did not know you felt. Watershed events offer shortcuts through the journey to belonging. Only at a moment like this, when the America you had thought invincible lies bleeding, can you find yourself overcome by a surge of unexpected emotions. For a sample of unexpected reactions by immigrants at the time of national tragedy, see Box 2.

BOX 2
The Case of Haghnazar X

Haghnazar X was a seventy-five-year-old retired school principal from Iran when the World Trade towers in New York City were attacked. Though he had lived in the United States for nearly twelve years by then, he still dreamed of his birthplace. He lived on the fourth floor of an old apartment building in Forest Hills, Queens. On warm evenings, he went to the balcony, where he kept several pots of red geraniums. He turned his gaze to the horizon. In the great distance he could see a slice of Manhattan's skyline. Each time he looked at the horizon through eyes that were clouded by old age, the cityscape appeared like that of Tehran. In this melancholic reverie, he sat sipping tea, composing poems for his lost city.

On the morning of 9/11, Haghnazar was watching television when the news of the attack broke. He could only see a blurred view of the mayhem on the screen. Because his English was poor, he always muted the sound when he watched American television. But on that day, he did not need language to know a disaster had befallen the city that had taken him in. He stepped onto the balcony to look around. The skyline was obscured by rising smoke. His heart sank at the sight. Something took him over. He got up, turned off the television, and went to the dollar store around the corner. When he returned to the balcony, he moved the geraniums from the railings. He had never been one for flags, never owned or bowed to one. But at that moment, all the nevers had died out in the urgency of the flames. The co-op board did not allow exterior displays, he knew. Yet the man who had not dared break any law before committed the first illicit act of his life. He draped the biggest American flag he had been able to find from the railings. He was overpowered by an unexpected tide of grief for America, which had, until that morning, seemed invulnerable to him. As he silently stared at the billowing black cloud, he wept for the dead. But he also felt an affection he did not know he had for his adopted homeland, and he wept for love, too. Tehran, he realized, was his muse. New York, on the other hand, was his home. The darker the sky grew, the more clearly he saw on which side of that sinister smoke he stood. Years later, Haghnazar X always said of 9/11 that it was the day that his immigrant gratitude gave way to a patriot's love.

American memorials celebrate the deceased with song and fond recollections. Eulogists speak with affection and humor about the dead, even make the attendees laugh. There is usually music, too, sometimes a chorus of beautiful songs. An American funeral is rarely a stage for hysterical displays. If the nation's most notable figure dies—say, a president—they will not drape their public buildings in black banners. They will not ban music on the radio or laughter on the streets. Government offices and schools will not be shut down to mourn the death of "the Leader." Yes, flags will fly at half-mast. There will be mounds of flowers, candles, and stuffed bears at the gates of his residence. Trained dogs will be around for the bereaved to pet. But there will not be throngs of men beating themselves, striking chains over their shoulders, or howling until they are faint and breathless. To express sorrow, no one will make himself bleed. No one will throw himself in the way of the coffin as it is lowered into the ground. Instead, bugles will be played. Americans grieve stoically. Watching them mourn a loss is often a somber but dignified affair. Their ceremonies are meant to calm, not to incite more tears and sorrow. Does this soothe the mourner more? Perhaps not. But it dictates to the forces of living to resume their reign and overcome those of doom and inertia.

The American zest for life can certainly be infectious, but it can also be worrisome to the immigrant. You may realize that you had prepared for every manner of death and sacrifice but no form of actual living and forethought for a future. You were always too busy getting through crises. You could hardly think beyond the next day or two. The past was always far too present, and the present was fast in the grip of lingering grudges against the past. Besides, most of the time you were solving the problems of survival. If you had dreams of a better life, it was not because it was expected of you to have them. It was because you were an ambitious optimist. You did not always know how to get there. You placed your bet on luck and hard work. Between you and that nebulous future, there was an escape via a lucky visa or a high score on a major test. But just as you may find unexpected spaces opening up in your mind in a few years, and even purchase a pair of binoculars, you will also learn to fill your calendar with events to come. You, too, will begin to imagine yourself growing old and contemplate retirement, which you had never thought you would live long enough to reach.

THE VICES AND THE VIRTUES
OF AN AMERICAN LOVER

The people who make so many plans as if death is never coming do not think it is ever too late to fall in love and start again with someone new. In your former homeland, nothing would have signaled madness or disgrace more than remarrying, in your fifties and beyond, after a divorce or the death of a spouse. Here, on the other hand, nothing can stop an octogenarian from marrying another octogenarian. In fact, they will be praised, their names announced on the morning news broadcasts as models of vitality. Perhaps Americans think that if they live life so unequivocally, death will hesitate to come along. Whatever the reason, these national penchants for bird-watching, tree-tending, future-planning, and self-caring make Americans more likely to be attentive lovers. In a society where sex consultants have their own talk shows and freely dispense on the airwaves words that would have had them and those listening to them arrested in your former homeland, where psychologists brazenly write regular columns on how and whom to love, where a man and a woman do not have to show proof of marriage to rent a hotel room together, love, among other changes, undergoes a slowing process. In these circumstances, love's fervent boil has a chance to turn into a simmer. The autonomy the two lovers have to make their own decision without family or community bearing down upon them, the space the society grants them—the freedom to hold a lover's hand, feel a lover's touch, see the lover's face, walk and talk with the lover in the park without the fear of neighbors, nosy relatives, or morality police—lessen the heedlessness that accompanies the love that is under prohibition. Restrictions have a way of intensifying passions. If in your birth country love was a tornado, wild and all-consuming, in America it can become a lovely rain. The urgency of the crises that eventually uprooted you often impelled you to take leaps of faith, express emotions before they had perfectly ripened. There was no physical plague to drive people into desperation, but a political one that made every day seem like it could be the last. Chaos and uncertainty made time seem scarce and all experiences ephemeral. That is why human bonds formed more easily. Tears flowed more quickly. Hearts filled with affection more readily. Invitations to a home-cooked meal came after a first pleasant exchange. Tight embraces—which take Americans months to ease into—often followed a mere warm greeting in the past. In America, where the circumstances do not force you to say a quick "I do" or lose the lover, when families no longer press and rulers do not regulate people's intimacies, love can behave sanely.

The advice Americans give to a newly dating couple is, "Take your time." Indeed, why rush in a country where the national project is to extend the present to last an eternity? And take their time they usually do, going through the stages of American dating: (1) a daytime coffee, (2) lunch, (3) predinner drinks, (4) dinner, (5) invitation to a nightcap inside the home of person A or B, (6) a sleepover, (7) professing love (or a solid hint at it) or exchanging vows of exclusivity, (8) meeting the respective families or close friends, (9) moving in, (10) planning the hows and the wheres of making a dramatic proposal, (11) engagement, (12) wedding.

You might say it took God half as many steps to create the universe and ask why American courtship is so prolonged. The answer is that freedom's great gift is time and willfulness. They give Americans their special air of confidence. Even the greatest critics of America describe it as the "sunny" quality of Americans, or their so-called can-do attitude. By this point, you might be growing anxious, thinking that you have missed out on too much in life. If so, this may be a consolation: their prolonged courtships do not guarantee success. American marriages often break up for the exact reason that America herself succeeds. That strapping self, so vital to intellectual inquiry and personal achievement, will not easily get fitted into the bounds of matrimony and parenthood. To be a spouse or parent at times requires the reconfiguring of one's inner architecture, shrinking or dismantling certain internal spaces to retrofit oneself to the requirements of family life, something that every "self" is loath to do.

In the marital language of your past, a loved one might

be addressed by very serious terms like "my life," "my soul," or "my breath." Here the marital language is lighter and more palatable—"sugar," "honey," "sweetheart." The intervention of love consultants, wedding planners, how-to-propose instructional videos, relationship columnists, and bridal magazines with their photo spreads of barefoot couples chasing butterflies in the meadows raise the expectations for a marriage to impossibly high levels. A spouse is supposed to deliver the other to some version of a conjugal utopia. The nation that invented Superman does not always know where fantasy ends and reality begins.

There is also the matter of the perennial difficulties inherent in marriages. Some prefer to contend with loneliness than to deal with the stresses of togetherness. Americans have a strong aversion toward discomfort. The marketing gods have many people convinced that they must own far more than they really need in life. Rather than a pair of sport shoes, they feel that they must have a pair of shoes for every sport. A knife here commands far less respect than the knives you used to know, because the American knife has to compete with a zester, peeler, corer, slicer . . . Perfectly good rags land in the trash, because feathery dusters and high-performance microfiber cloths have elevated dusting from a mere daily chore to a form of domestic combat.

While marriage to an American can be complicated, a love affair with an American can be worth the trouble. To begin with, there are genuine "I love yous" in America. The "I" that has been groomed for so long will unequivocally assert itself— eventually. The admission will not come as quickly as admissions or emotions might have done in the past. This is partly why the easy kisses, embraces, and other expressions of affection you might have generously doled out before ought to wait, lest they be called "over the top." At first, you may take "over the top" as a compliment, thinking that you have outdone yourself, surpassed the proverbial bar. You will be stunned especially by the antiseptic echo of "over the top"'s sidekick, "inappropriate," which could offend you. A similar warning can sometimes come as "You're too much!" to which you may be tempted to say, "You're not enough." Such a feeling on your part, if aroused, is justified. Despite the popular use of effusive phrases like "more than happy," Americans tend to be guarded, even frosty, and could do with a bit more warmth and breeziness of expression. Yet you must resist judging them and your early experiences. If you do not, you will take the easy way out, throwing your hands up and saying to yourself that you cannot "understand *them*" or "get along with *them*." Be warned that this would be an exercise in the "Law of Immigrant Inertia," the force that keeps you from discomfiting interactions, which, if overcome, will lead to smoother assimilation.

The slothful American "I love you" will come late, but it will come with clarity. Love here presents without symbols and metaphors. You may come from a tradition that was rich in love but sparing with the admission of love. Or perhaps love manifested itself less in words and more in other ways—in heaps of homemade food, endless expressions of anxiety, boundless generosity. Love fed you, serenaded you, fussed over you, recited poetry to you, worried for you, and gave up much for your sake in time, money, and opportunity. You gleaned it in the lavish meals that were spread, services performed, or sacrifices made on your behalf. But sacrifice is often a prelude to guilt. Love, then, became bondage. This business of giving oneself up for the good of the child, spouse, or parent trapped the beloved. One generation lived for the next and expected those offspring to repay their debt in adulthood. In the end, so many came and went without anyone living their own dreams, only continuing the love-shackled existence of the ones who came before.

LOVE'S NEW LANGUAGE

Just like love, lovemaking, too, has its own language here. If you come from a culture where all the words for sexual parts were considered obscene and no conversation about sex could be had without resorting to vulgarity, you are in for a treat. English will offer a wide-ranging lexicon, including a respectable one, to talk about what could once only be spoken of in unappealing ways. From puberty to menopause and everything in between, through the use of humor, illustrations, scientific charts and graphs, and all manner of clever ways, Americans have created an industry to speak about the unspeakable. Like the birds, and the trees here, too, they have named every part—large and small—and every sensation to create the unabridged dictionary of, er, sex! Some of these words you knew, but not all. As certain subjects that were taboos in your culture may not concern Americans—the notion of virginity, for instance—the words associated with them have lost their currency and disappeared from the lexicon. And so some words you knew from the past will not be in the American vocabulary. If you are, say, a Persian or Arabic speaker, you will find no synonyms for words like *gheyrat* or *namoos,* both of which implied a man's duty or honor in protecting a woman's virtue. Some notions have yet to exit in the society you have left behind, which is why you will not find the word "privacy" in either language. "Private" is there, as in something owned by someone—i.e., a car, a wife, a house, by a man. But the word "privacy," as in "You cannot walk into my room without knocking first," does not exist. How could it? The individual who should be able to demand to have privacy has yet to come into being, and so privacy has no conduit to carry it into speech. Similarly, because this culture does not ask men to be the keepers of women, the English lexicon has no synonyms for an adjective that glorifies a man's protectiveness toward the family females, or his show of valor in guarding them against other men. In short, the words that are missing represent the underlying beliefs that are missing, the ones you have left behind. And in this particular instance, good riddance to them!

The English erotic terms may not be all that appealing, but at least they are utterable. If you happen to find the right partner, lending an ear to them can set your imagination, and much else, on fire. This bedroom English will not be of much use elsewhere. Still, practice is practice, and what better training than one-on-one, and what more conducive a classroom than a warm and plush setting? In short, this is cultural immersion at its best.

With time, both the unappealing and the appealing words

will pass your lips. You will grow fond of "I love you." You will eventually know its buttery glide on your tongue. "I love you" comes so effortlessly to Americans of all stripes and in every context—from the printed patterns on panties in lingerie shops to finger-painted artwork made at daycare—that you could say the words are perennially in vogue. The abbreviated version of it can sound perfunctory, but with a simple tweak of the tone, you can fine-tune it. Say it as you stare into the eyes of another, holding each other's hands, and there can be no mistaking its romantic charge. Say it as you laugh heartily after hearing a friend's joke, and it no doubt captures the spirit of fraternal gaiety. Say it toward the end of a long telephone conversation and it stands for the gentlest of sign-offs. Speak the words with enough suppleness and you could pass for an American. Someday you will carry on full conversations in your mother tongue but at the end switch to English to say "I love you." When you are comfortably fluent, you will be unchained, able to express yourself without awkwardness.

To get there, you would do well to woo an American. For a woman from a misogynist land, this may well be an imperative. All your life you have lived inside a cocoon, unaware of your own potential. An American lover could help give you wings. Contrary to what you had been told about the moral corruption of Americans—their "promiscuous women" and their "depraved men"—you are safer now from predators than you were before. While America is still an unequal society, women are far better off here than where you used to be. You might wonder how the legal and social privileges these women enjoy manifest themselves in a liaison. For starters, your opinion will be asked for, from the seemingly small—"Merlot or chardonnay?"—to the large, which may have to do with your preference for what sort of intimacy, if any, should follow the merlot or chardonnay. Does this mean no harm will come to you in the hands of an American? Not one bit. It only means that years of public debate about the rights of women and protocols of consensual sex have heightened the general awareness about what is good conduct and what is misconduct. So you are more likely to experience yourself not as a lamb in the wolf's maw, but as a shepherd guiding your flock. A sumptuous thought! An American love affair ought to go as smoothly as a car ride on American roads. Unlike in your former homeland, where drivers and pedestrians treated traffic regulations as mere suggestions, here they are set in proverbial stone. A "no" here is as good as a red light against what you find distasteful, and a "yes" means proceed. However, while one "no" ought to instantly stop whatever needs stopping, two yeses can be an invitation to proceed at a faster or more intense pace, and three, even more, and so on, and so ecstatically on.

In the absence of all the official and unofficial busybodies who kept watch over you in the past—not to mention God and his self-appointed lookouts—here taboos stand a chance of falling away. Your American partner is less likely to feel squeamish around your body's natural cycles and more likely to think of pleasure as a currency whose value grows when exchanged. As you hide less—be it inside your clothes or timidity—and apologize less, you will find shame washing away like dust from a window after a good rain. Here, where the family or tribe no longer decides whom you will marry, you are free to choose any mate you wish, of whatever background, or even gender. You may find yourself wanting to break from the vows you had once been forced into taking, to start anew. It will be difficult but possible. Anything you never dared imagine is imaginable. But first and foremost, you must learn to imagine. You must get to know your body, not as the inconvenience it once was, but as your chief instrument of living, a vessel that, if you cherish it, will deliver you much pleasure.

Your American lover will likely explore your body, study its perfections and imperfections. You might at first think this a sizing up of sorts and take offense. After all, every immigrant arrives with at least one suitcase and several bundles of insecurity. But what you are mistaking for an appraisal is really a carnal "meet-and-greet" hour. Whereas in your birth country the standards of attractiveness may have been tightly defined according to the preferences of a mostly homogenous lot, in America there is little consensus over what is sensuous. The commingling of so many people here has created a vast range of different looks. Just as your palate will in time grow more sophisticated and you, who were born in, say, Turkey and raised on *kofte*, might develop a daily hankering for Korean *japchae*, so might you find yourself wild about an Ethiopian. The American term "the sky is the limit" is a metaphor for ambition and the vertical possibilities for personal achievement. But there is no metaphor for the possibilities on that other axis. In America, one's eyes get an advanced education and begin to appreciate the looks they had never beheld or thought they could find appealing. Beauty comes in so many shades here, thanks to the many nationalities. If in your birth country you were the proverbial ugly duckling, chances are in America you will be thought of as unique and exotic. You see, the marketing bosses have cultivated among Americans a certain hunger for all things new, different, and even slightly odd and unfamiliar.

Your knowledge of sex proves to have been woefully limited. You had imagined it a businesslike affair, a physical give-and-take, unfolding in a set of predetermined acts. But here, with the right partner, sex will be play. So much so that there is an industry producing toys and other accoutrements to facilitate the fun, publications to guide and arouse, virtual communities where the private can become less so. You will discover that your body can be something unlike what you once knew. The former autocrat's most elemental exercise of control was to disrupt the relationship you had with the material life, starting with your body. Once he achieved that, and you lived without desire, everything else followed. Your body became a mere inconvenience, a beast to tame and treat ascetically, a nuisance with needs you had to satisfy, a machine you had to feed when food was scarce, or keep cool or warm when neither was possible, keep clean when disease abounded. Your body had always worked against you. Now it is no longer a wellspring of anxiety. And if you get to know it, it can at times give you delight. Lie there and be caressed. A lover's attention may finally let you know your body in ways you never have. You will experience pleasure where you had not thought pleasure could burrow.

Here, where the morality police do not bang on the door, the neighbors cease to snoop, the veil falls, and shame follows suit, the body is the blank slate for all manner of joy to register upon. This is what an American lover might well show you. He may not like his looks—his bald head, his flabby torso, or his squat figure—and yet with him, there will always be a way to love, or simply be together, no matter the circumstances.

YOUR FIRST ROMANCE:
A FEW WARNINGS

Before you embark on your first romance in America, be sure to cleanse your mind of all old unsavory ideas, so that your heart can do what a heart must. The men here are not philandering drunkards, and the women are not unanimously promiscuous. America is not where virtuous women go to be misled and corrupted. And, no, these women have not been holding their breath for you to arrive. To simplify the matter, here is a list, which for ease of reference you can think of as the Seven Deadly Sins, Immigrant Edition:

> 1. Permissionlessness: Never assume a woman is asking for "it" because she is, according to your cultural standards, dressed provocatively. You are only required to be respectful and gentlemanly to her. Never assume a woman has given you permission to lay hands on her unless she has explicitly said so—no metaphors, similes, facial gestures, smiles, or nods mean the same thing.

2. Misbegotten Manliness: Never fear that wearing certain clothes will make you appear less "manly." Manliness is not a role you play and does not have special lines or props. You need not avoid wearing shorts, tank tops, or short-sleeved shirts. The measure of your manliness is only in your conduct and character, not in your choice of colors or haberdashery.

3. Mistreatment: Never assume a woman needs any less or differently than you do, or that Americans are less affected by poor or bad reception than you are, because you somehow believe that they feel less than the people of your ethnicity. Also, if you previously had resentments about America—objected to U.S. foreign policies, still do, or have unsettled feelings about America as a colonial power—rest assured that your sexual conquest does not qualify as righteous vengeance or justice. Copulating in the name of a higher cause will not advance that cause.

4. Self-Delusion: Never return to your country of origin to find a spouse to bring to America. Do not think that an imported wife will be a controllable wife. She might be obedient for a while and behave according to tradition, but not for long. Once the American oxygen fills her lungs, she will feel light and take off. To a girl handpicked from a queue in the old country, you will never be a beloved. You will only be a ticket out of her

unhappy life. Do you dare get sick or fall frail alongside such a person? Be wise!

5. Foolish Stoicism: Never assume silence is a sign of strength or that having a heart-to-heart with your beloved is unmanly. Or worse, never assume that by keeping silent you can make a discomfiting matter go away. A vast self-help industry relies on the nation to believe in the necessity and the power of "talking about it." If you do not talk, you may have to submit yourself to couples or family counseling. Given the stigma against psychotherapy in your community, and the risk of you becoming a laughingstock if you do go to a counselor, learning to talk may avert loss of reputation and save you from disgrace.

6. Small-Mindedness: Never assume that the woman whom you enjoy in bed cannot be the woman you marry. A woman's virtue is not lost if she takes and gives pleasure. If there ever was a troublesome divide that did not need to exist, it is this. You *can* love and live with the person you enjoy intimacy with.

7. Misplaced Honor: Never assume your honor lies outside of you. In the past, it may have been lodged under the garments of the women of your household and tied entirely to their conduct. If the women of your family behaved as tradition dictated, your honor would

remain intact. If they wore revealing clothes, disagreed with or defied their fathers, brothers, or husbands, or showed the slightest interest in the opposite sex, they would dishonor you. But honor cannot be so fickle as to readily slip away with someone else's misbehavior or be restored with someone else's "good" conduct. Invent a new brand of honor, one that springs from within you. Better to be without the kind of honor that would have you forever bossing others.

SIX

The Diaspora

Can't Live With Them, Can't Live Without Them

Find out if your relatives want you
before you start for America.

—CECILIA RAZOVSKY,
What Every Emigrant Should Know (1922)

One morning, you awake to realize that the days of homesickness gave way to weeks of melancholy, and the weeks of melancholy turned into months of dread, and the months of dread
became the seasons, then the first year, and then years of separation from all that you never thought you could separate from.
There is no beating around this bush. The journey to America
hollowed you out, but has it filled you up, too? Inside, there is
a gnawing that you cannot articulate. Anything you might say
to describe it will sound strange, like: *The ground on which I once
stood is now askew.* Puzzling, but true.

THE ABRIDGED CATALOGUE OF BELONGING

As appearances go, you look like you have gotten on fine. There are many ways you might realize that you are no longer a helpless newly arrived immigrant but an established resident instead. It may happen when you cannot remember the date according to the calendar of your former homeland. Or it may happen when a coworker leaves on your desk a newspaper clipping about the recent elections in your birth country, and reading it you do not recognize any of the candidates. Or it may happen when you refuse to stomach a nosy relative's prying into your personal affairs and demand that he respect your privacy. (At hearing this, the relative will jeer, "Privacy? Good God! You've become an American.") Or it may happen when, standing in the cashier's line at the supermarket, you see that your old coin purse is now a formidable wallet, bloated just like a proper American wallet, its every pocket stuffed with a credit or scan card, all qualifying you as a first-rate consumer, the gold standard of assimilation. This plastic inheritance belongs to you, who did not have a single card when you arrived. Or it may happen, most dramatically of all, in an encounter with plainspoken new arrivals from your birth country. In them, you see your fresh-off-the-boat self, and in you, they see their own future. Nostalgia draws you to them. Fear of becoming permanent exiles like you drives them away from you. Meeting them brings home better than any other experience how far you have come, which in their eyes, at that moment, is too far.

Such an encounter can happen in many ways, and this may

well be one: You are shopping for foods of your cuisine at an ethnic store. In the frozen meats aisle, you see a couple quibbling over a package, looking as flustered as you used to look during your first few weeks here. You beam a friendly smile as they approach. In a tortured English they ask if you could help read the label. Greeting them in your native tongue, you put on your glasses and take the vexing item off their hands. Their brows smooth in relief and they instantly begin to chirp. From the way the wife tightly clutches her handbag in which she keeps their passports—she refuses to leave them in their apartment—you estimate their time of arrival to be no more than a few weeks. The husband shyly confesses, "We came *out* six weeks ago."

He means to say that they "left" the country or "arrived" in America six weeks ago. You find this endearing for it reminds you of how, in those early days, the only *in* is the land you have left behind. Everywhere else is *out*.

You welcome them magnanimously, assuming the air of the self-appointed mayor of America. The wife, whose eyes glisten with tears, corrects her husband and adds, "Six weeks and four days ago."

"When did *you* come out?" the husband or the wife will inevitably ask, hoping to find company in their post-arrival misery. You will tell them. Then you add, ". . . and four days ago." You have not kept count of the days after all these years, but you want the woman to know that you understand the toll it takes.

Hearing your answer, the husband, fully animated, stabs the air with an index finger and says, "You're one hundred percent an outsider to the country now! You know nothing about what anything looks like there," he says harshly, as if you are a carton of milk that, having been left out for too long, has soured. "So many new roads, you couldn't find your way around without a driver. The homeland today isn't the homeland you knew!" Being new to exile has inescapable side effects. In some, it manifests as the unkind treatment of those with whom the uprooted feel a kinship. They turn both on the country that they feel rejected by and their countrymen, too. In exile, it is their turn to reject.

The wife, slapping her cheek, would similarly exaggerate and say something hyperbolic like, "I'd be dead if I stayed here for ten years!" These are the illusions that most immigrants nurse in the early days, when they are full of longing for home. It helps calm their fears of a permanent rupture with the past. It occurs to you to say that certain senses in you are, indeed, dead since you arrived, but you choose not to make the point. They are new here; there is no need to bury them deeper under their heap of grief.

You say nothing. Your silence goads the husband. Suddenly Houdini, he claps his hands together and blows into the air to animate the vanishing of all the things you knew and says, "Since you've been outside of the homeland, all's changed. Nothing stands as you remember." Then he adds, "But you still speak the language well! Good for you!"

Something snide rises to your tongue. Curb the urge to say it. It is not he but what he has touched in you that will make you angry. Not only are you hopelessly out of your homeland, but he has shoved you to the margins of your heritage, too. *You still speak the language well. Good for you!* The punk! It angers you because this is, in fact, one of your nagging anxieties. Sometimes you wonder if you belong anywhere anymore. With his brusque gestures, he has banished you from your birthplace, reduced you to a mere outsider, irrelevant and suspended. All the fears you had never made sense of finally make a new reality clear before your eyes. Your tribe now is the tribe of the Nowhereians. Only those close to you who remain in the homeland insist on claiming you as one of theirs, and that is mostly because they rely on your remittances. Those who need nothing from you do not hesitate to disown you. Among Americans, however faint your accent or solid your mastery of the culture might be, you are always from elsewhere.

You might be naturalized by now and have an American passport. If not, you have a travel document, which really means that your home, at least officially, is an existential no-man's-land. It implies that you dwell in a twilight space where your hold on the past has loosened though your grip on the present is not firm either. Yet your two compatriots standing before you in the market see you as red, white, and blue through and through. You must choose your final words to them carefully and say something dignified, such as you, too, never imagined staying in America for as long as you have, but the years did not care what you imagined. They passed. Then you must turn your attention to what got the conversation started in the first place. Read the printed lines on the label for them, describe the ingredients, then hand the package back. It is best not to linger. Leave them there, in the cold of the frozen food aisle and their inadvertent cruelty.

THE GOOD IN DIASPORA

Not all encounters with the diaspora are hurtful. In fact, you live in your community, even now that you no longer need to, because in it you find the warmth and camaraderie you have yet to find elsewhere. Decades may pass and the enclave still remains the same as when the first wave of its immigrants had established it. A slice of your people's history has been preserved on a few American streets. You like walking around these blocks, where every English store sign appears alongside its translation in your native language and some do away with English altogether. You like seeing Americans go into the grocery stores and buy the foods of your cuisine or frequent the local eateries featuring the dishes of your childhood. You might not be the begrudging sort and yet, when you see this, you cannot help but think to yourself, *Aha! We're not such a burden on the system after all.*

There are things you have learned to do but do not love doing them, like tolerating the taste of peanut butter, or shooting the proverbial breeze, which according to the American code of conduct makes you a prized conversationalist. You have adjusted to so many things that jarred you at first, including their inches and Fahrenheit. Some things you still judge severely, like the presence of a gun store next to the pizza parlor and the dental clinic. Some things you have learned to judge less severely. You now simply walk past the soap and candle stores, which you once thought of as monuments to American frivolity. You do not shun bars, but instead have grown to love their dark smoky air in which strangers bond together through the blessed influence of alcohol.

Still, some things puzzle you—chief among them baseball. Years have passed and yet you do not get baseball. You cannot bring yourself to call a real sport a game that involves a ball so tiny that it is invisible from the bleachers. Sport? Nine players putter about while only two do some throwing, swinging, and, sometimes, running when they are not fussing with their gear or making mysterious hand signals. Nevertheless, you rise to your feet with others and chomp on sugar-crusted peanuts for the sake of harmony. Doctor's visits, too, have never shed their oddness, with all the release and consent forms that you sign without reading. America has many perfunctory announcements, including drug warnings at the end of television commercials that are spoken too quickly to be heard or understood.

Some road signs fill you with pride: "Littering $250 Fine," though it does make you wonder about the wisdom that led to such an exact number. Other signs are still riddles to you: "Rotary Club Meets on First Monday of Every Month." You do not know what the Lions Club or the League of Women Voters is, though they sound harmless enough. You have not wrapped your head around the denominations among churches and not advanced beyond Catholic and Protestant. You still do not know to call animal control when you see a dead deer on the side of the road and are not sure what the difference is between a selectman and an alderman. You still prefer to pay for things in cash and hesitate to take a loan from the bank. You were raised to distrust all manner of borrowing. You buy only the things you can fully pay for, or you do not buy at all.

You are mostly content, though it is not to be confused with a state of complete happiness. The hardest by far for you has been learning to live with a heart that is not beating to the rhythm of some perpetual foreboding. To learn to go out in the morning and look at the sky, and then turn to a strolling neighbor on the sidewalk and say, "It's a beautiful one today!" You have finally understood that running is no longer what you do when you are chased, but a healthy and enjoyable exercise.

Several times in these past years you saw, met, or heard something that made clear to you why you gambled so much to come to America. The thought has occurred to you after a few rare and earth-shattering experiences, which were followed by equally earth-shattering insights. You were walking through a foreign airport where everyone else stood in one endless line and U.S. citizens breezed through, as if the plane had landed you there, and now the blue passport, your American magic carpet, carried you through the rest of the way. Or, say, you and your fellow medical doctors in training were in a meeting, discussing a very sick patient. The doctor in charge gave an overview of the case, then turned to you and asked your opinion: "What do you think is the best course of treatment now?" A thunderbolt might as well have struck you. There you suddenly were in a world where your opinion was sought. You were too stunned to speak. You hemmed and hawed, then said a few inarticulate words to the chief, but the real lesson you drew had nothing to do with the patient, his sickness, or medicine at all.

You were speechless because it suddenly was so clear why you had to leave your birth country. Yes, you liked America's drive-throughs and roller coasters. But the reason you left and can never return is about all that this moment had given you. You had been respected as an equal and knew that from then on you could never go back to a place where you would be treated otherwise.

And yet you cannot explain why with all the wealth of possibilities that America has bestowed on you, you are still in the firm grip of loneliness. Even when the buds dot the bare branches and the spring flowers bloom in their full glory, there is something frosty that does not lift from America. The warmth of the old life and its simple ways do not exist here—something that your expanding closet or the growing trunk space in your new car cannot make up for.

You used to be without so many things you now have, but you did not feel so alone then. This is America's greatest mystery. You have probably gained a few pounds since you arrived. Many newcomers do. But in spirit you are lighter than you have ever been. Like candy, you too came in different flavors once: hard and tart outside of home, and when inside, soft and sweet, though tinged with the day's sour goings-on. Each day that you ventured out, you camouflaged yourself so as not to draw attention and chance getting stopped, questioned, arrested, abused. You walked more stiffly and purposefully then. You kept an eye on who followed you and who was ahead. You steered clear of anyone in a uniform, even a traffic officer.

These days, you have shed that jittery persona. You are carefree and pay little attention to who or what is behind or ahead. The old foreboding you had each time you set off from home has lifted. You saunter now. You have developed a liking for wandering, if only to discover new places. Sometimes you pause to pet a passing puppy. You have mastered the American art of making canine conversation: "How adorable! Is it a he or a she?" You also know to ask permission before laying a hand on that venerated fur, and to exercise curiosity: "What breed is he?" Above all, you know how to say all this naturally. You do not let on that you come from a place where all dogs were nameless mutts that paced the streets of your childhood. You will not cringe when a friend's dog sits on the couch at your side, its saliva dampening the velvet fabric. If the neighbor's dog dies, and you see him go by without a leash in hand, you know that you must put on a somber face and stop to say that you are sorry for his loss. The nation that invented individuality extends selfhood to its animals and anoints them each. The wonders of America . . .

Years will pass and you will become so many other things. A father, mother, grandmother, or grandfather, doctor, engineer, lawyer, cook, shopkeeper, dancer, producer, priest . . . You may lose your accent altogether. There may be no traces of the past in you or upon your life. But you will, whether you speak of it or not, always remain the refugee, the immigrant, the one who crossed into the new land. You do not understand why because your bout as a trespasser may have been short-lived. But no matter. It will define you, as much as if not more than anything else. Inside you, one stream of blood is flowing in your veins.

Another is of memories of the crossing, beating against the mind—equally warm, equally vivid. It is what you will whisper in the ear of your lover one night, after you have confessed your love for each other. It will be what you will confide to your grandchildren. It will be what you tell every time you wish to bare your soul to someone. There is no intimacy unless the story is told. So the telling becomes an act of bonding.

Despite the many years, you remain spellbound by the grandeur of America, above all by the mammoth one-story wholesale stores—the warehouses of her abundance. You may not have a large family, or any family at all, but you still buy a few things there. Other people look into counseling or meditation for inner peace, but you wonder if they have experienced the curative qualities of a stroll down a Costco aisle and the contentment that springs from seeing six tightly wrapped cans of sardines for the price of only one at the local market. Being able to drown yourself in so many staples at such affordable prices is an American miracle—one that is made possible by China. You prefer this no-frills setting to luxury stores. The spare presentation of the goods, the exposed, unadorned displays. The bag-your-own policy captures so much of your personal philosophy: practicality before appearance is the guiding principle here, with a sampling of precooked meatballs on the side. Show and tell, like the bazaars of your past.

You shop at your neighborhood ethnic stores, too, for entirely other reasons. You go there to eavesdrop on some of the daily dramas that had animated your childhood and still, though less and less, unfold in this neighborhood. The newly arrived walk into these stores, fill their baskets, then walk up to the counter, ready for a good haggling. It is a dialogue you can script even before it begins:

SHOPPER: This fish . . . how much?

SELLER: Seven dollars and fifty cents a pound.

SHOPPER: Seven dollars and fifty cents? Highway robbery! Next door, they're only three ninety-nine.

SELLER: These are the freshest in town. No frozen, God-knows-where-they-come-from imports here.

SHOPPER: Freshest? These?

The shopper sniffs the fish and wrinkles his nose, then pokes the creature under its gills and goes on.

SHOPPER: This thing has been dead longer than my grand-father, may his soul rest in peace.

SELLER: Then go next door. Shop there. Let the line move!

SHOPPER: No need to get fussy . . . how about four dollars and fifty cents?

SELLER: Madness! Four-fifty is below what I paid for them myself. Next customer!

SHOPPER: Okay. If you want to be stubborn about it, fine, seven dollars and fifty cents. But throw in an extra.

SELLER: Look, this is America. No extras or bargaining here. Prices are fixed. What you see is what you pay.

SHOPPER: America, America! This is America! Fixed prices is all you learned from America. How about the customer is always right?

There will be sighs and grumbles, but money along with due cordialities will be exchanged before the doors shut.

In lieu of haggling, once the most satisfying aspect of any shopping experience for your fellow expatriates, they have embraced the exercise of "returning," which might well be haggling's fair-haired twin. On weekends, they load their spacious trunks with the purchased goods they plan to return, something that was unthinkable where they came from. At first, they even return the things they need, just to see if they can. When disbelief gives way to faith in the sanctity of the return policy, they begin to return only what truly needs returning. They had expected to see the suspension bridges, the underwater tunnels, the endless forests, and bottomless seas. But it is the exercise of returning goods that is the surest sign of America's greatness to them. The experience of an underwater tunnel lasts only a few minutes. However, the experience of a trial sweatshirt, whose price tag scratches against the nape, lasts for days. It is why they cherish their receipts and keep them alongside other well-guarded family treasures. Returning items is the proof that the consumer, one of the several manifestations of the citizen, is formidable here. It is the evidence that anything is possible because a one-time decision need not be destiny. You can change your fate here and turn it in for a better one. Taking the oath of allegiance is a rote promise. To stand head high at a customer service counter, receipt in hand, turning in an unwanted garment is an actual step toward claiming one's rights, acting as an entitled citizen would. Even after all these years, each time a reluctant shopkeeper takes an item back, you stagger out in awe,

praising God and His most unsung messenger, George Washington. This is one of the many small joys of living in America
that only you, privileged with a keen knowledge of despotism,
deeply cherish.

There are oddities about living in your congested enclave.
It is there that some childhoods come to a sudden halt. Some
daughters must mother their mothers who are at sea here, some
sons become their father's scribes and interpreters. Parent-
teacher conferences become parent-teacher-student conferences, as you might still need your child to translate what the
teacher says. There is a lot about the American school you cannot know, but some things are clear: Your kids come home less
exhausted and without a headache, because there is less noise
in the classroom, which is significantly smaller than those they
attended in the past. They are also less listless at the end of the
day, because they had a meal at school. It will be years before
you learn of the shortcomings of this education system, but
for now it is one grand miracle unraveling in stages—first you
learned that the school was free, then that the school bussed
your children for free, and finally that there was a daily lunch
for free. You want your children to get from school all the things
it has to offer, except the irreverence and apathy of their native-
born peers. They must understand that even though America
is now their home, the children they should emulate are their
fellow immigrant students, not the Americans. In the summers
and on weekends, in whatever business you start, the children
will become its human pets, infants crying in some back room
of the nail salon, teens staring at an iPad in a sweltering kitchen,

their faces blurred behind the steam of sizzling woks, or napping on piles of rugs in a furniture store.

You will walk your children to their schools and see their laboratories, libraries, and auditoriums. Your child may turn to you and ask what your school's theater looked like and what shows you staged. It is best to say that your school was very different and not burden him with the facts of your past at that moment when he feels proud of being your guide. But telling him the family's odyssey is surely essential as he begins to think about who he is and what he must become. If your children are too young for school, they will go to daycare and return home sick, which is how you will catch the American viruses you had escaped until now. Whereas they will recover swiftly, you remain in bed for days thereafter. Their American childhoods will stir bittersweet feelings in you. You will read the puffy bath books, the illustrated books, the pop-up books that you never read and discover the world of joy that this nation has invented for its youth. If the thought makes you sad or wistful, it is because comparisons between your threadbare childhood and theirs can only lead to envy. Remember that your kids need not only be the small people whom you raise. They can also be the conduits of your second shot at a proper childhood, your chance at redeeming the past.

You do, however, have a permanent complaint about your children, though they might otherwise be fine little people. They, alas, do not speak your mother tongue. They listen to you but answer only in English. It has become a battle of wills. You keep speaking it. They keep not speaking it. Can you blame them? What is the joy of your mother tongue other than the bad news that airs on the shabby exile television stations, broadcasts that are the soundtrack of your living room? They all try to sound and look like their American counterparts but mostly fail miserably. If it is not the anchors with their sorry programs, it is the cranky relatives and grandparents who camp at your house for days on end and forget to behave like guests. They think scolding the kids is part of the grand tradition they must keep alive: Don't talk back to your elders! Don't be loud! Pull down your skirt! When they do not scold, they boss the children, sending them to fetch things—that, too, they justify as a cultural education, anything but their own slothfulness. These commands kill the joys of the language you want them to speak, and you somehow miss seeing the obvious. You also forget that you are up against the dazzling lineup on American television, a universe of the most alluring characters and gripping stories. Instead of pitting yourself against English—a losing proposition—try to instead introduce the joys of your own mother tongue and the magic of intimacy it grants you and them. This may require that you teach them some things that are unseemly, coarse terms a mother is always telling a child not to use, but it will be worth it. For instance, your language might be particularly rich in synonyms for, say, flatulence and its nuanced variations in scent and sound—something that English does not have. Vulgar? Yes, but it is the only way that you can stand a small chance against the allure of Cinderella and Spider-Man. These particular expressions will allow you to show them how your mother tongue can be their secret language, a way of carrying the small world inside the home among the strangers outside. It will also make it more possible for them to access your past and the cherished though tragic place you ran away from. It allows more depth in the future conversations that you will have with them about the homeland you may no longer be able to visit. For a sample conversation between a refugee mother and her American-born children, see Box 3.

BOX 3

A Car Ride with Two Dissident Parents and
Their Very Young Children

Lin and Lou X, two former student activists from Hong Kong, were driving home from a family wedding when one of their five-year-old twin boys in the backseat asked the question they had long dreaded.. Lin drove as Lou caught up with work on his mobile phone. It had been a long weekend of festivities, where the twins met their extended family for the first time, crowded on the dance floor with their newfound cousins. Chasing each other through the wedding hall, they would stop to steal a bite of something delicious as they ran. They enjoyed the attention of the relatives but were left puzzled, too. The other children had all gone to China already, where most of the original extended family lived. They spent summers there and bragged to the boys about their visits—the loving relatives, the outings to amusement parks and zoos. It was something the boys had never done, nor could they hope to, since their parents, two political asylees, had been targeted for their activism by the government. Now, as Lin spied on them in the rearview mirror, they were busy whispering to each other. From what she could hear, there was a squabble unfolding. The first brother urged the second, "You say it!" and he resisted, insisting that the other should. At last, at a red light, one of the boys blurted, "What have you done, Mama?" The question came in the same accusatory tone he had heard adults use when he spilled juice on the furniture. The second brother chimed in with a question of his own. His voice was laced with rebuke for the mother whom he was certain had done something so bad that she had had to flee to America to hide. "Why can't we go to China, Mama?" Their smooth brows were similarly knitted as they gazed at their dubious mother. How had she shamed them? Robbed banks in Shanghai? Pirated ships in the South China Sea?

When Lin asked what they meant, the boys said that other children had told them that China was just another Disneyland, a place full of fun, and that if their parents had been good, they, too, could have gone back. The idea made Lin both furious and heartbroken. Furious because she had done nothing wrong. In fact, despite all the ordeals she and her husband had suffered, she was proud of what they had done together. Heartbroken, because she hated to think that anything she had done, honorable though it was, had somehow upset her children. China was not the magical place the vacationing cousins had described, but how could she convey that to her small boys?

The light turned as she stammered an answer. She was not willing, or ready, to tell them of the dreariness of life under tyranny and the nobility of those fighting it. For a moment, she thought of the easiest answer: "Someday when you are grown up, you'll appreciate what I have done." But it was not Lin's way to condescend to children and imply that they were somehow not capable enough to understand. Of all the unpleasant fallouts from her activism, Lin had never expected that her own twins' disappointment in her might someday be one. When she tried to explain why China was not the land the other kids had described, the boys glared at her in disbelief. The irony was not lost on her: on one hand, her former compatriots in China think of her and her fellow activists as corrupt agents of western influence. On the other, Chinese expatriates in the United States treat her as "trouble" and keep her at a distance. In truth, she had not been a member of any party, nor did she aspire to any political office. For most of her adult life in China, she had been a journalist, sitting behind a desk almost every day, often in her pajamas, and writing for several hours in a solitary room overlooking their bustling neighborhood block. It is hard to imagine why or how any government could possibly be threatened by her. Yet they were. She found the most direct explanation to tell her boys, "They don't like what I write."

"Well, Mama, why don't you stop writing things they don't like?" one boy advised.

Lin thought about all the things she had lost since arriving in the United States: her friends, family, her university community, the youthful hope that she could rise up to make her country a freer and better place, and, finally, China itself. It was irrational, she knew, but she could not help the wave of emotion that overtook her as she thought her boys were the next things she was going to lose. That day in the car, she resolved to do something more than merely raise them

to be healthy and hardworking boys. That was no longer enough. They also had
to be boys who would always see the truth even through the propaganda and
the façade of prosperity. She would raise them to believe in their mother's cause,
however unsuccessful she had been, and be proud of her history, and claim it as
their own.

TO BE OR NOT TO BE: IN THE ETHNIC ENCLAVE

The familiar ethnic ghetto, for all its reminders of home, is equally a reminder of the limits of America. Years have passed, and yet here you might still be in the same community in which you first arrived. Kinship may have brought you there, but one of America's many ceilings may be keeping you from getting out: the glass ceiling for women, the white ceiling for nonwhites, the bamboo ceiling for Asians. You worked hard from the first day you arrived. You learned English quickly and were at the top of your class all through high school and college. Yet you will not do as well when you enter the job market. No matter how qualified, you will not become the CEO of the company where you work, or the chief at the lab where you do research. Your merit and diligence carried you all the way through university, but not beyond. Your mistake has been to abide by the rules of your former land in the American workplace. You will not speak up at staff meetings, lest the boss think you disrespectful. Rather than sounding like the proverbial squeaky wheel, you are quiet, because you were always told not to trouble other people or draw attention to yourself. You exercise modesty and never toot your own horn. You have been told from childhood that you must put yourself through "bitter labor" and wait for recognition to follow. But here, it will never come. In the eyes of the American boss, modesty is not a virtue. It is often taken for incompetence.

Or you may remain in the congested enclave not because you have failed elsewhere. There is safety in living there, which is not to say that there is no danger. Only that this danger is the kind you know. Familiarity is a potent drug. It does not cure, but it often comforts. Dozens of tastefully built and decorated American cafés are nearby, with cheery young baristas who will ask what they can get for you before you reach the counter. Instead, you go to a compatriot's dive, where the tables wobble, the chairs never match, and the walls, save for a few sun-faded airline posters of your birth country, are bare. Here the owner is the same as the barista, who is the same as the server, the busboy, and the cashier, and none want to take your order, not eagerly anyway. Only when you do order, no one will say the ghastly "I beg your pardon?" You might not hear anything particularly welcoming, but you will not have to repeat yourself either.

Do not chalk up this ease to language alone. There is more at work. You have grown fond of English, now that you speak it well enough. But having to still be mindful of so many social details does put your head in a straitjacket. It is not just the words you must find and say at the right time. It is also the right stretch of smile that needs to follow those happy words, a well-timed nod in agreement, a furrowing of the brow when speaking of confusion, all of which give you the air of an insider. You might as well be in charm school, walking with a heavy book on your head when you do this kind of talking. But in this ugly café, you bear no loads. You can just be and replenish the warehouse of the ears with the echoes of your native tongue while listening in on conversations around you. If you remain here too long, you will miss your American friends. You even miss being an American. And if you stay among them for too long, you will miss this drab hole, which is filled with lost beloved things. There is no remedy for this. This is the gift and curse of exile: a bifurcated life of slight but permanent discomfort on either side.

At a corner table, there is usually a posse of elderly men, huddled together. They claim to have once been movie stars, generals in the royal army, leading scientists with dozens of patents to their names, or wealthy businessmen with several confiscated factories and mansions. Outside of their homelands, all exiled professors are a bit more professorial, the generals decorated with an extra star, the formerly well-offs turning tycoons upon landing. Exile truths are somewhat exaggerated and all exile exaggerations hold kernels of truth. It is easy to disbelieve this particular crowd, slouching against their canes, age spots dotting their skins, sweetening their coffee with generous helpings of sugar, for they have seen enough in life to be able to reject all medical and nutrition advice. In a country where success is a national aspiration, sitting alongside people whose titles begin with "former" is comforting. Stripped of all glory, there is little hunger here, only the smell of smoke, the steam of drinks, and the reminiscences of what was and can never be again. You ought not to readily doubt that these men were once great. They do not look like stars because certain lights do not cross borders well. They have mostly come here to live their final years in peace and to die in peace. They escaped a death by torture and imprisonment, or by an explosion of a mine underfoot, or a shoot-out in a gang war, or hunger or heatstroke while walking in some no-man's-land. Americans may fear their odd speech and strange headgear. But they have come in pursuit of the same quiet life some fear they are here to disrupt.

THE BAD IN DIASPORA

Still, if you linger among your compatriots for too long, the old irritations will set in with little prompting. It takes only a rendezvous with one of them to bring on the frustrations of the past. You plan to get together at, say, four p.m., and he walks in at five, all smiles and without concern for why you seem in a tizzy. Lately, when you throw a party with mixed guests, you send out two sets of invitations. One for the Americans with the real start time of the festivities, another for your compatriots, with a start two hours earlier. Your people are always delayed. Appointments meant little in your former homeland. Where the laws protected the powerful, every rule or convention was something to resist or defy—punctuality among them. Why be on time in a land where the future is, if not bleak, then at least uncertain?

This also explains why you would suffer the hassle of walking through the congested ethnic enclave rather than driving on its streets. Traffic laws did little to direct the flow of vehicles where you once lived. They were the only laws the citizens could safely break to express their discontent with all the other laws that oppressed them. Drivers honked incessantly if frustrated or ran a red light to show spunk. Nothing else embodied the full sense of the mayhem in your homeland better than a popular intersection at rush hour. Why would you obey the laws that did not protect you? During your first days in this neighborhood, you might have ventured to drive. But soon you saw that you could be moving at a good speed down a busy avenue until suddenly the car ahead would slam its brakes, only to greet a pedestrian on the opposite sidewalk. A boulevard could be six lanes wide, yet there will never be more than one lane open in either direction as cars double- and triple-park along the way, oblivious to regulations. On the highway that passes nearby, your countrymen have been seen in the shoulder lane backing up to the exit they missed. Why go through the inconvenience of driving to the next exit when the right one is just a few feet behind? America prohibits the import of many products from other countries. But no amount of metal detectors, police K9 dogs, or dour immigration officers could stop your compatriots from importing the traffic chaos of the old country into the new.

What they did not bring along, they most ably adopted, among them some of America's sinister practices. In the shop windows, on street benches and billboards, the faces of your clean-shaven and formally clad compatriots gaze upon the passersby. Some are real estate agents, looking giddy and aglow under floodlights, others are attorneys appearing stern and well-fed. In your native script, the first group claims to know the address of your dream home, the second promises a hefty compensation for the injuries you do not know you have suffered. In this particular part of America, the rule of law has yet to be embraced, but the rule of lawsuit has.

Some of these residents are only physically in America, while their thoughts and preoccupations are stubbornly elsewhere. They cannot name their state senators or congressional representatives, but they brood over the elections in the homeland they will never see again. On their computers, nine of the ten open tabs will be websites in their native language. The tenth will display currency exchange rates. Their radios are on all the time and tuned to the news of that other country. Their exile-produced television broadcasts air talk shows, though "show" is a generous term to describe a program made, filmed, and hosted by the same person. There he sits, the former famous anchor from the homeland in front of a camera no one is operating, in a bare storage room with only a plastic ficus tree for decor. He talks ad nauseam or takes phone calls from people who talk ad nauseam, and sometimes, when no one calls, he answers personal calls on his cell phone. Seeing a former star fall so low, the exiles have yet another reason to seethe.

They also seethe when remembering the pensions they can no longer collect after all their years of labor. They spend hours plotting schemes to avenge themselves—so many hours, in fact, that they often forget why or from whom they wished to get revenge. For these stubborn few, America is only a temporary home, though they will see eventually that they are to live in it permanently. If they can dodge paying taxes, get paid cash under the table, they do. America has not wronged them, yet in the bitter bookkeeping of displacement, they do not care from whom they borrow as long as they can get even. Telling the truth, living according to the rules, behaving as a citizen should are not innate skills similar to seeing or breathing. Rather, like walking and talking, they must be learned.

At the entrance of each store, piles of magazines display dozens of advertisements for all kinds of services, some truly essential—such as wire services for sending remittances to relatives—others disguised medical and insurance schemes urging you to *DIAL NOW.* All manner of elderly assistance and facilities abound, where native-speaking doctors readily order an MRI and an EKG if an aged compatriot walks in with a runny nose. All this crookery will be forgotten within a generation. Once the community trusts in its place in America, the memories of these dark beginnings pale. Whereas the second generation will be fully rooted here, the first generation, yours, always dreams of going back: You will become a doctor, then go back to cure the poor and the sick. You will become wealthy, then go back to revive the broken economy. You will wait long enough and the regime will fall, then you will go back on the shoulders of cheering crowds, hailed as a hero. You will become a U.S. citizen and go back to claim your confiscated property. No matter how long you live here, in your mind, you will always be returning. There is one way to stay in America but a thousand ways to return home in the imagination—in anger, in regret, in longing.

It is hard for native-born Americans to work among these newcomers and make sense of their disorderly ways or not be horrified by their dubious practices. Just as you had to master English and the ways of life in this country, so must the Americans who choose to do business in this neighborhood study the atlas of its suffering. A social worker, for instance, will be stunned to find that his clients did not tell him the truth about their income, or the amount of rent they pay, or whether they are able to work. He takes their lying as a personal offense. He does not know that lying for such an immigrant was not a question of deceit, but of survival. In the old country, that immigrant had been a Scheherazade. To be spared another day, he had to tell a lie every day. He lied from the morning when he left his home until he returned. He lied even without speaking. In his office or shop he sat under the image of the president or the Leader he loathed but had to pretend to love, or he stood in a queue mouthing the words to an anthem that he did not believe in. If he was a policeman, he stopped a car that was traveling at the speed limit and, to collect a bribe, threatened to issue the driver a ticket for speeding. Or if he lived in a country under prohibition, he secretly bootlegged beer or wine to get by. Or if he wanted to get access to free internet where the web was censored, he spent hours finding a way to break through filters. And though the latter is not an example of lying, it is a prime example of how the good hours of a good day were spent trying to get at the truth. In short, truth had been so elusive and obscure to the immigrant for so long that he may not know how to do without lies. It will be a while until his spirit airs out in freedom, unbinds and expands to its full unafraid capacity. That is when he will no longer diminish himself with lies again.

THE IMMIGRANT'S AFFLICTION

While living among your compatriots, you may find the haggling, chronic lateness, dreadful driving habits, billboards with their sketchy ads, even the lies are only irksome. They hardly affect you, not because you are impervious to them but mostly because you are not around enough to be affected by them. You work five days a week and, if the opportunity arises, you work overtime and on weekends. If you run a business, you keep the doors open seven days a week. If you are a scientist, you are the only one in the lab who knows the cleaning crew on the graveyard shift. If you are a nail salon worker, you rub the fetid feet of customers who would otherwise feel no other person's touch, much less at the end of a long day when other businesses are long closed. If you are a caregiver—a babysitter or an aide to the elderly—you do your best to generate genuine emotions at the rate of twelve dollars per hour. You do not even go home at night; you live in the same quarters with your charge and sleep the sleep of a sentry, drowsy but on guard.

What is there to do if not work? As you get over the early hurdles of arrival—settling in, learning English, finding a job—the hardest task of all begins to loom: how to go about the business of living. How do free people live? What is the shape of a day that is not fitted between the hours of official curfew or electricity outage? What is a night without fear? What is one that does not end at sundown because bars, discos, music, dancing, and gambling are not banned, and lasts as long as your legs can carry you? When you pictured yourself living in freedom, you did not give a single thought to its possible snags. In the absence of the despot and his restrictions, how do you define who you are if not against *him*, and what is your purpose if you no longer have to depose anyone?

Now every small step requires a decision you must take the trouble of making. The old restraints helped you know exactly who you were *not* and what you did *not* stand for. You never had a reason to think about who you *are* and what you are *for*. You were so busy resisting the archenemy that you did not imagine a day when resistance would be over. The fury you used to feel had you fired up. Here in the land of liberty, the fire no longer burns, and you must admit that your dictator kept you far more alert than your morning coffee ever could. Compared to the daily agitations of your past, America feels like a convalescent home. No one had ever told you about the adverse effects of freedom: it can cause confusion and laziness.

Do not search for all these answers in your mind. Begin with your body. Embrace Americans' goal of living a long life. The specter of an impending sacrifice on behalf of the Leader or the faith had you believe that your body was only a tool, a weapon in a grand struggle. Well, the struggle is no more. Educate yourself in the ways of joy. Sign up for some salsa lessons. Try a scuba diving class, or anything else that will focus your attention on the material world and show you some of the experiences you never knew existed. Going into the woods with a pair of binoculars could be a good start, too.

If all that reinventing proves to be too much, keep punching the time card twice a day—your new curfew—until you find your answers. You may only be here to work, to send your kids to good schools and provide for them in your home country. You call and text them daily, injecting your presence into their days, but you know it is an illusion. You are not together. And it is possible that you never will be. Still, a regular paycheck lessens the burden of separation. Having few things never bothered you before. But now that you know how much there is to be had, you care to have more. Work is your life—your drug and your drink. Work is what you drown yourself in to numb the pain of loss. Work pays, and the pay sustains those you love. From thousands of miles away, an "I love you" is too evanescent, no more lasting than smoke. The words dissipate into the air as soon as you speak them. But a solid pair of sneakers on your child's feet will last long after you hang up. You work so you can love. And to love generously, you must work a lot. The more hours you work, the more exhausted you get, the more love you can package to send. You may not even need to work as much as you do, but it seems like the thing to do in America.

Do all you must, but remember this awful truth: even with your every effort, and the efforts of the loved ones you left behind, you may still lose one another in the end. Few loves can withstand the wound of separation, despite the shoes and the endless professing of love. For most, distance works like acid to dissolve the bonds. Sometimes, the distance may be traveled together and the old bonds still do not endure. Marriages fall apart upon arrival. Wives who had tolerated the mistreatment of their husbands are no longer inclined to do so in America. Husbands whose wives had been chosen for them by the clan learn the allures of falling in love and choosing for oneself. You may have left because the miseries you faced were breaking the family's back. Your exit was the best remedy you could think of to help everyone. But like all remedies, it solved some problems while creating others. By the time you are all reunited, if you are ever reunited, you may not be the same family again.

Imagine, then, being divided on two sides of the oceans and cataclysms—war, revolution, despotism, disasters—scarred by separate tragedies, burdened by separate memories, transformed by separate stresses, then having suffered through everything without the presence of the other. Under these circumstances, most relationships will experience a rupture, and feelings of abandonment cannot but ensue. Afterward, you might not want, or be able, to reunite at all. To be separated by borders causes far less despair than to be separated by bitterness. The one who remains behind grieves the loss of the one who is gone. The one who leaves must overcome the yearning to return. If the former succeeds, he will remain steadfastly the same, because to be the same is to keep what they had intact. If the latter succeeds, he is likely to have changed. Only by changing could he quell the homesickness that paralyzed him in those early days. Building a new future may well require forgoing the attachments of the past. This is the choice the lone immigrant will face. He must toughen up. He must shut away memories and loves, so that he can move nimbly forward. Cruel? Yes. Essential? Indeed. Emigrating does not just uproot the person. It uproots the heart, too.

Such a person is likely to suffer from a lifelong case of a

broken emotional thermostat, an immigrant condition in which the afflicted cannot quite regulate the intensity of his attachments. The fear of losing everything again will be hard to overcome. He may not know how much loving is too much or not enough. He may warm to others too quickly and intensely, or not warm at all. He may show affection when in the proximity of new acquaintances, but it will all fade when they are gone. He will not do again what he once did—yearn, write letters, make calls, and wrestle with the beast of absence. He will always find it easier to let everything go, turn his back on what he cannot keep, and break his own heart. He prefers to be unfeeling than to go on longing.

These scars and maladjustments make up the worst of your insecurities. They also give you good reason to stay among the diaspora. Your compatriots know and expect the afflictions of their own kind. There is no need to pretend around them. The comfort they offer, though, often comes at the price of having to live with the cruel rules they have brought along. Old misbehaviors resume, sometimes more firmly than in the past, as if to make up for other former severities that America prohibits. Patriarchy, for one, spreads like a bad weed even in the new country. Your religious clergy will still walk to your doorstep demanding that you attend daily prayers. They want you to live in the America that they design for you—where you live the same oppressive life as before, only in a different climate and with more reliable utilities. The older you get, the more difficult it will be to leave your community, and the more you wish you could return to your homeland to die. America is a place to be young in, but not one in which to grow old. Besides, you can string the English sentences together when you are well. When you get sick, the English words go from your memory like good health from your body. Your enthusiasm to speak the language fades with age, just as the spark does from your eyes.

If you are a girl in a conservative family whose comings and goings are closely monitored, school may be your best exit strategy. Do not hesitate to go to a faraway college, if you have the option. The farther you get from home, however besieged by hardships you might be, the greater your chance to become a woman of your own. Whispers will abound about how America corrupted you, how you were seen shedding your headscarf, walking with a boy, dressing provocatively, or disobeying your elders. There is no bottom to the rumor pit in your community. Forgive what you can and get as far away from them as possible. However distant, their gossip will still reach you, but at least you do not have to greet them and feign delight at seeing them in the neighborhood. Return to them when you have made something of yourself. Only then will they gather about you, each telling their own tale of how they always knew you would become a somebody, and how they urged you to pursue your dreams. They will act as if they have never done or said otherwise. But remember, nothing wipes clean the slate of memory as well as success.

THE UGLY IN DIASPORA

One of the knottiest predicaments that living in diaspora may present is America threatening war with your former homeland. The hostile rumblings will come before the war itself does. You may turn on the news and hear the announcer say in a highly starched tone, "This afternoon the president signed an executive order banning travelers from six nations to the United States." Hearing this, you will gasp. Since your arrival, you have been dumbfounded by many things American. Some have been significant, like the rampant lawsuits that pit brother against brother or the arsenal of weaponry in some ordinary households. Others not so, like the all-you-can-eat buffets or the water glasses brimming with ice in frigid February. Yet you overlooked them. When it came to serious matters, you always trusted that America would not falter. Now you know that she can. The nation that has lost its sense of proportion—from supersizing its french fries to overmedicating its sick—is ripe to exaggerate or overreact to the threats against it. One night, you go to sleep a lawful resident or even a citizen. In the morning, you wake up an outlaw. And yet, that is not the worst of it. The worst is that every bit of confidence you had accumulated about your place here will fall away. You will return to who you were before coming to America. Your earlier life taught you how to cope with hostility when the tide turns, and in America the tide can seriously turn. It did for the Japanese Americans during World War II.

You had once mastered the sad art of living under tyranny.

After all, you were conceived in a banned world. You grew up listening to bootlegged CDs delivered to you by smugglers. You watched banned movies. At parties, you drank banned drinks. You read banned books and magazines, which you had to bury under the flowerbeds in your backyard. In your former homeland, the authorities would barricade mountains and cordon off seas. They would drain the rainbow if they could, because it shone with the bright colors they had banned women from wearing. All this is to say that when America bans someone like you who has fled a life of prohibitions, she simply returns you to what you know. For so long, you had to figure how to outdo, outlie, and outsmart bans to get by. Censorship runs in your veins. You know how to edit a line to pass the censor's muster, stay under the radar. And that is what the label of banned does; it strips you of your sense of belonging.

They want to go to war because the rulers in your former homeland are dangerous. But they also say that they fear you, you who had to flee your homeland because its rulers were dangerous. You ran away to live in safety, not to inflict harm upon others. You and your fellow citizens were the first victims of those rulers and know better than anyone how dangerous they are. Every morning, at the entrance of your high school, guards checked your bags, not looking for weapons, but for forbidden books or music. They sniffed every girl, not for the trace of drugs but the illicit use of perfume. They raided your parties and celebrations, lest alcohol was being served. They locked up writers and journalists for the crime of not falling in line with the Leader's commands. Every right that was taken away was taken

away in the name of piety or safety. But if you were safer, it was
because you were living less. You only tiptoed around the edges
of life as if it were a fearsome beast not to be awakened. You
wish you could tell America that to undo her covenant with the
likes of you is to unmake herself.

THE END OF CAKE

You may have left your country because you were opposed to
its regime. Or you may have no interest in politics at all. It will
matter little. You will always be asked if you are, say, North Korean what you think about the current standoff between *our* two
nations. Those who ask this think themselves wily for trying
to ferret out your allegiances through "inconspicuous" inquiries.
Unless you are a member of the opposition against the government in your former homeland biding your time to return as a
minister or some such, you will not like the question or have
a simple answer to it. You may have left precisely because you
wanted never to think about North Korea again. But when the
war drums begin to sound, your success at forgetting the past
will be as likely as the success of the hen forgetting the maraud-
ing fox. The birthplace you left will haunt you. There was nowhere to hide from the Leader when you were there, and there
will be no place to hide from the troubles he brews, not even
in America. His sinister schemes, which almost always include
a mad arms race, will fixate Americans. The threat of a nuclear
war will be on the radio and in the newspapers. It will flicker
on the monitor when you browse the internet. At first, it will

only be in the headlines. Then, as is always the case with things nuclear, it proliferates. There will be panels on the evening news. Pundits will spout on cable television, with their charts and graphs. Intelligence agencies will weigh in with their figures and send their footmen to the evening talk shows to duke it out against nuclear-minded others, who will exercise their own special nuclear math and nuclear forecasting: *How much uranium must be enriched? How many centrifuges will have to spin?* You used to think about books and after-school programs when you thought of the word "enrichment." Not anymore! Enrichment is lethal now. The threat of a nuclear confrontation will turn many once innocuous things into alarming ones. Yellowcake will no longer bring cake to mind. Yellowness itself could stir ominous feelings. Every place of calm or reason will brim with foreboding. Inebriated men in small-town watering holes are most dangerous. If they get wind of where you are from, a beating could ensue.

You might decide to get away from the news and do something wholly apolitical, like go to a poetry reading at the local library. But there you will find that lyricism, too, can no longer exalt. If one of the presenters happens to be from North Korea, an audience member will raise his hand during the Q and A's to ask if the poet thinks his country will attack America. Once the words are spoken, every verse and every other thought will vanish in the mushroom cloud of fear. Yes, even poetry can become radioactive.

AND YET, IT CAN BE WORSE

None of this should surprise you. If it does, it is because there were signs you ignored. In the last presidential race, for instance, men in suits lined up before the cameras. Among the topics they debated was the threat from your people and how a war was long overdue. Their opinions varied, but everyone agreed that immigrants from your nation, and refugees in general, were a threat to America. In their administration, refugees would be more severely vetted or barred altogether, they all said, and then nodded in unison. You dismissed this because you found it laughable that a lot who had never been uprooted, queued up against the fortress of a U.S. embassy for days, been vetted or barred, could ever succeed at painting you as dangerous. As the men verbally bundle you along with thousands of other immigrants and refugees from faraway nations, you find that you have new brethren. You feel bonded to them, you see yourself as one of them, a citizen in the nation of wanderers. Something about those months in transit has become as ingrained in you as all the rest you had once been or have become.

Do not ponder any of this for too long. If you do, you might begin to feel sorry for yourself, convinced that you have been hexed by a double curse: the first because you were born where you should not have been, and the second because you came to a place where the specter of the first would give you no rest. So what are you to do? It is simple. Learn from your new countrymen: Move on! Buy that pair of binoculars. See if you can spot a yellow-bellied sapsucker. With a little luck, by the time you do, the focus of the news will have shifted to other disasters.

And what if your country is involved in an American war? For one thing, you, too, will lose your peace even in America. In your own solitude, the clamor of war persists. The turmoil penetrates you. Against the backdrop of war, all that you had thought or hoped to have forgotten will wash over you. You lost everything when you left. Watching the bombs fall, you lose them all over again. You had once bitterly wanted to have revenge, to see the land that had expelled you explode. But not anymore. Watching its grounds shattering, you realize that the land had always been only earth, and blameless. The rage you felt when leaving had been a savage rage. Distance and the tranquility of the past few years parceled it into something less poisonous.

You will do nothing else but watch the news. The questions you dread others might ask are the ones you are asking yourself: *How do I feel? Whose side am I on? Is it about sides? Who do I hate? What do I hate? Do I hate? Or do I hurt?* You may have no relatives in the war zone to worry about. A relief indeed! Worry, however, is only one emotion. There is also grief, confusion, and the anger that still remains. There is, above all, that lingering longing in you despite the years. You think you miss your motherland. But what you really miss may not be a place but an experience. For instance, you may have lived through a time when your nation overthrew its tyrant. You watched the euphoria that swept over your country. For a short while, the dictator was gone, and it seemed that freedom had finally dawned, and that no despot would ever rise to power there again. Now you know you were wrong. You also know that no wound endures longer or stings worse than the wound of lost hope. What haunts you is not the country. What haunts you is the young idealist within who, wistful about the bygone freedom, has a better hold over you than the adult.

You watch the news of the war all the time. Then one day, you click on a new link—as you have been clicking every other day before that—and a scene appears in front of your eyes. The picture is unsteady. The camera is in the hands of a person who is running. In the middle of a large square ringed by dried, jaundiced grass, two men are climbing a statue. You examine the image and recognize the statue. This is your old square, where your father used to take you for ice cream on summer afternoons. You would sit together on a bench, watching the cascading fountain. Water sprayed your cheeks, cooled your faces as you relished your treat. Once in a while, your father looked at you and shook his head from side to side to express his pleasure at everything. "Eden, Eden," he would mouth, since the roar of water drowned all other sounds.

You move closer to the screen. The pool is dry, its cement bottom bloated in some places, cracked in others. No vendors or children are in sight. The men reach the top of the statue and drape a banner over it. The banner falls, and so do your tears. You cry because, along with the grass, your most cherished memories have withered, too. Your father's Eden is desecrated. Even *you* can hardly picture what it once was in that arid fury.

You might conclude that there is nothing worse than America declaring war against your former homeland. But, alas, there is. It is for America to do nothing when a war breaks out in that homeland. Your nation might be torn in two, violence raging in its every corner. Yet, in the name of peace and respecting the sovereignty of other countries, America will stand by and watch. At first, the news of this war will make the headlines. After a few days, it will be relegated to the inside pages of the newspapers. Within a week or two, it will get no mention at all. Months pass. Thousands die and even more are displaced. You feel enraged while most others seem oblivious. Once you were powerless because you lived in a dictatorship. Once again, you are powerless, this time in a democracy. Until now, you believed you had come to a mighty country that would defend the weak. When you first arrived, the administration that was in power vowed to support your people if they rose up against their dictator. Years later, they did. By then, a different administration pursued a different policy and would only help your people through "thoughts and prayers."

It can still get worse. And this is how it will come about: You wake up one morning and see on the news the tyrant you fled from standing beside the American president, shaking his hand. You rub your eyes. You have had bad dreams before. You look again and the two are joined in a handshake, flashing their media grins for the reporters. The voices of the pundits narrate the images, hailing a peaceful diplomatic solution to a long-standing enmity. There is even a mention of peace prizes for the two parties. Diplomacy, you learn, is another term for an exercise in large-scale deception. In this brand of diplomacy, other nations have their own "traditions." In the name of culture, the diplomats turn a blind eye to everything reprehensible and befriend tyrants. They treat the arrest and imprisonment of writers or execution of gay people in your former homeland as a domestic matter. Freedom of speech and assembly, fair and free elections, and equal rights are only the materials of eloquent speeches. In practice, the president who is shaking the hand of your dictator clearly does not think other people need them, too.

When this kind of diplomacy is in full swing, you and the rest of the diaspora face a reckoning. The America you knew will come to an end. As its leader goes on "normalizing" relations, you and your compatriots will lose your safe haven here. Some members of your community cope through forgetting. They may have spoken strongly against the tyrant before, but not anymore. Instead, they will say that they have lost interest in politics. Now they only care about art, culture, and literature. No longer organizing marches or demonstrations or soliciting signatures for petitions, they will plan galas to honor your ancient civilization. They arrive at ballrooms in their ostentatious cars and their ostentatious gowns. They have mastered the aristocratic glide and move smoothly from person to person, introducing one to another, clinking their champagne glasses. Turning a deaf ear to the ongoing abuses in your homeland, they now speak only of cultural heritage. Dead kings will become all the rage. There will be awards named after your former monarchs, presented with such fanfare that the thuggery of those who run your nation today will be overlooked. Merchandise featuring your historic ruins will become fashionable. Ancient royal emblems and insignias will appear on bow ties and dangle from earlobes. To the diaspora, the old ruins become a "cultural" matter that they passionately embrace. The new ruin that is your real homeland today, however, is a "political" matter, something for politicians to deal with, not for culture lovers. You seethe. For the foreseeable future, seething is all you will do.

What you do not know is that a dictatorship has a half-life. When it is new, it is thought of as an evil the world must rid itself of. But if it is not toppled in time and goes on to endure, the next generation will likely see it as just another imperfect regime, and you as merely bitter and unforgiving, too old to see anything from a fresh perspective. You insist on remembering the history others wish to forget. In short, you become a nuisance. You and your fellow exiles bear children who want to discover their "roots" and return to their ancestral land. They wish to go on short visits, see their relatives for a week or two in the summer. The children go as malcontented Americans and return as third-world enthusiasts, with newfound identities. They turn against their parents for having left at all, for denying them their heritage and a loving extended family. The children do not know that much of the charm they hold for those relatives is in their very American accents and upbringing. They have no clue that if they safely travel through foreign airports, it is because their U.S. passports with the gold seal are as good as bulletproof vests. The overflowing love they get from the relatives whom they have not seen in years, or ever, is genuine, to be sure. But even the relatives love them, in part, because they are American novelties, whose visits are welcome for being short-lived. They always return to the comforts of America. Nothing in the world can cultivate an appreciation for distant cultures as much as the safety of American citizenship. Their parents, on the other hand, are immune to the charms of the old land. For them, America, only a way station for so long, is at last an irrevocable terminal. When the relations are normalized, and their dictator is recognized as legitimate, they know that they can never return, and will forever remain American.

When diplomatic relations resume between America and your former homeland, the Leader who so far had affected you only through the news has a freer hand than he ever did. He sends his goons into your enclave. Or, for the right price, some of your compatriots might decide to become turncoats and work for him. You can no longer trust anyone. Everyone will become suspect. Most tyrannies are content to rule within their own borders. But yours is not most tyrannies. It cannot stand its enemy, even after it drives the enemy into exile in foreign lands.

In the past, when America thought of your tyrant as you do, you could rely on her to stand by you. But the new diplomatic ties change that. Between adhering to principles and staying at the side of the dissident immigrant and your people's demands for democratic rights and the rule of law, or forsaking everyone and everything for political considerations, America will, alas, always choose the latter. In short, you must brace yourself to be sold out by America at any moment. She has many virtues, but patience and steadfastness are not among them. Which is why certain American tragedies recur, no matter how much time passes, and certain lessons are never learned, chiefly that all

U.S. citizens—Christian and non-, native-born American or naturalized—are created equal. See Box 4 for an early example of a naturalized U.S. citizen who was treated as a lesser citizen.

BOX 4

The Story of Hajj Sayyah

In December 1874, Mirza Mohammad Ali, nicknamed Hajj Sayyah, a globetrotter from Persia, sat before President Ulysses S. Grant as his guest in the White House. The moment was historic, for it was the first time that a Persian citizen was meeting an American president. Though for most of his life Hajj Sayyah had been no more than a highly curious and otherwise destitute traveler, many world leaders assumed him a nobleman and hosted him at their courts. So it was that Sayyah, who had been to the Ottoman Empire, Central Asia, North Africa, East and South Asia, and Europe, and learned six languages along the way, had even been received by the pope.

But his visit to the White House was not like any other visit, because for Sayyah, America was like no other country. He had decided that of all the places he had seen, America was the only nation that truly recognized the dignity and the rights of the individual. Enamored of the Bill of Rights and the individual liberties granted to the citizens, he imported American ideals to his native culture by coining the term "human rights" in Persian. It was because of all the affection and reverence he had for this country that when President Grant generously offered, "Ask me for something I can do for you," Sayyah asked to be granted U.S. citizenship. On May 26, 1875, his wish came true, and Sayyah became the first Persian American. Unlike many newcomers to America, he had not wanted America's riches. What he most wanted was to lay claim to the ideas upon which America stood.

Two years later, Sayyah returned to Persia. When he spoke of individual rights and liberties to his countrymen, few appreciated these novel notions. The king and his court found Sayyah's views "treacherous," and the religious establishment deemed them "un-Islamic." He was eventually arrested, charged with espionage for the United States, and sent to jail. When he managed to escape, he made his way to the newly established U.S. legation in Tehran, the precursor to what later became the country's first U.S. embassy. There Sayyah asked the interim ambassador for asylum. The ambassador examined Sayyah's naturalization documents, then wrote to Washington asking advice as to what to do about a U.S. citizen who had taken refuge in his compound. The response from Washington was sharp and unequivocal. Hajj Sayyah was not worth jeopardizing relations with the new host nation, for while it was true that he was an American citizen, he was, after all, only a "Muhammedan"!

SEVEN

The Loveable, the Inexplicable, and the Infuriating About America

The Americans are uncommonly intelligent. Their
minds are not given to abstract thought, nor are they
to be called a philosophical or imaginative race. But in
practical matters, in dealing with men and things as they
are, surmounting obstacles, and working out results, they
show a wonderful smartness, another word for ingenuity.

—AMERICAN SOCIAL SCIENCE ASSOCIATION,
Handbook for Immigrants to the United States (1871)

The more you stay in America, the less you know what or who
an American is. In your youth, you knew one kind of American,
the kind you admired on the big screen, the invincible ones
in the films who always defeated the villains and, no matter
how bloodied, survived to ride into the sunset with the girl on
their arm. Those are the icons who belong to any imagination
that would behold them. They are the reason why every child
anywhere in the world who raps, moonwalks, or dons a cape
hoping to take flight is a little American, too.

Later, when you began thinking of coming to America, you began thinking of Americans, too. You assumed "authentic" Americans were the ones with golden hair and fair skin. They intimidated you because you were convinced they were the country's true heirs to whom you had to ingratiate yourself, for this was *their* territory you would enter. Now, already in America, you have come to know a third species of American, one you never knew existed. This breed comes in a variety of complexions. You work with them, sit beside them on the subway, and stand with them in the cashier lines. They resemble none of the Americans you had seen or fancied. They do not behave as the country's heirs but its stewards as they go about the work of daily life.

More than any other nation, wild fantasies about Americans far surpass the everyday truths about them. Your former leader, an archenemy of America who issues lengthy sermons against the evils of American culture, has a Twitter and Facebook account and does not find this at odds with his preachings. He rails against the rampant consumerism of Americans, yet his children visit Europe regularly, in part to replenish their supply of Nikes and iPhones. No nation has ever held so much allure for others, was so secretly coveted yet overtly despised, or instilled so much hope and expectation along with fear and confusion at once. At U.S. embassies around the world, there have been sightings of former captors applying for visas, the very fatigue-wearing, Kalashnikov-wielding rabble-rousers who had taken Americans hostage in broad daylight before the news cameras. It is fashionable among certain ideologues and their supporters to hate America. Yet, as with all things in vogue, pragmatism always comes before vanity—a green card before a youthful anti-American fever. Making sense of this paradox has been your great task from the start.

A STRANGE BRAND OF GENEROUS

Some American behaviors shock you—for instance, the practice of "going Dutch" in restaurants. You cannot help but think back to all the times your former compatriots fought over the bill at the end of a meal and insisted on treating everyone. And here, they warmly share a meal for an hour or two, but end it with an anticlimactic examination of the charges and deliberation about everyone's dues. Americans do go Dutch, and yet they give in ways you might never have seen anyone give. This will puzzle you at first. All you see is an absence of generosity, because you will be looking for it in the places you used to know. Later, you will find something new, something unfamiliar yet dazzling. You might be walking into the post office absentmindedly one day when someone will hold the door and stand aside to let you pass through. The gesture will stun you, because you cannot remember the last time a perfect stranger smiled and held the door for you. Your countrymen hardly extended themselves to random others, especially not in government buildings, where everyone girded himself for the unpleasant encounter that was certain to come with the glum bureaucrat behind the gray counter. Many doors simply shut in your face as others ahead of you rushed in, paying no heed to who was behind.

Do you remember that very first night when you arrived in America? All along the road, you shuddered at the thought of having no one to help you. Then you stepped into your new apartment and found it modestly furnished. The local mosque had filled your cupboard with canned goods and prepared foods. The church had put in a dining table and a few chairs in your living room, and a bed in your bedroom. The synagogue had posted a list on your refrigerator of volunteers ready to tutor you in English and drive you to your appointments. Just as the feeling of gratitude was about to swell in your heart, mistrust overcame it: *Why all the kindness?* It will take years before you understand that here helping is not something one only does for one's kin. Americans do not help because you are one of them. They help because that is what they do. Through volunteerism and performance of civic duties, they honor their country. What bonds you with those volunteers who found furniture for you is not the sameness of your skin color, or your book of worship, or your bloodline. It is the sameness of the cherished American ground you now share with them.

For all these acts, they have a single name: "service." Serving others is to an American what celebrating the Leader was to your former countrymen. It is an act of patriotism. It is not through the practice of religious or ethnic ritual or the worship of a person, but through helping fellow citizens that Americans come together to care for the common love that is their country. It is through service that this jumble of disparate people join together as one nation. To many people, pride is a vice, something to shed or subdue. In America, pride is an honor one earns by refusing to be idle. Homegrown citizen groups, often made up of the retired elderly, invent their own ways of bettering their communities. They pick up garbage at the beach, guide visitors through the local museum, collect books for the library, stand in as big brothers and big sisters for kids in need, volunteer in national parks and fire departments, or go door-to-door to register new voters. Performing these tasks enables Americans to think themselves richer and more capable than they might really be. You may assume them heartless when they set a strict weekly allowance for their children, or expect them to provide for themselves once they leave home. But they are the very people who visit the local hospital and hold a lonely patient's hand twice a week. They ask you to bring your own drink to their dinner party, and yet they sign up to cook for the homeless at the soup kitchen. They do not give you a lift home if it might be slightly out of their way, but they will spend hours drilling the neighborhood Little League. And when a national disaster befalls them, they all come together like no other.

The world you come from had few riches to spare, let alone to bestow upon others. When people gave, they gave magnanimously, but hardly to the stranger. America, on the other hand, is the land of strangers who must bond through shared love. Here, perfect strangers often experience America's giving, and sometimes even anonymously. The first time you heard of a grant-making foundation, you suspected that it was a shady enterprise, perhaps a front for the CIA. Why would a person who had amassed wealth give it away to some random artist or researcher? Even learning of the tax benefits of such donations never fully convinced you. In time, you will realize that when the American self grows large enough, as the American self is meant to do, it sometimes acts as its own sovereign, setting its own rules where it can and advancing its own interests.

They teach their children to do the same. Their healthy, radiant teenagers travel to godforsaken villages on other continents. The adolescents most parents do not let out of their sight where you come from volunteer to build homes in the disease-ridden corners to which no airlines fly. They fill their bags with antibiotics and surrender their unblemished arms to the needles of many shots and vaccines. Off they go to "serve" in a foreign land, where there is no indoor plumbing. These children live among strangers who have never seen someone so young go so far from home to be with people who are not relatives. In the beginning, the hosts are suspicious of their young guests. When they eventually grow fond of them, they still think them, however endearingly, mad, or odd, or often both.

All these donors and volunteers have their own counterparts in everyday places, too. They are the waiters, clerks, and cashiers who, through their artful exercise of "customer service," have made the American shopping experience the envy of so many nations. The patty between the spongy white bun topped with the wilted orange cheese is not an American symbol by itself. It becomes so in the hands of a broadly smiling server who welcomes you to his counter. These servers say *Hello, Please come back soon,* and the particularly unctuous *How are we doing today?* Other nations produce goods. America's prime product is attitude, personal or otherwise.

Breeziness may only invoke a mere weather-related quality in foreign minds. For the American, it is the secret national attribute, with its most visible sign manifesting in the dress code. Informality owes its esteemed status to Americans, who readily dispense with the decorum that other cultures—bent on preserving the purity of their past traditions—will not give up. Here comfort sets the trend. The celebrated self dictates the terms of its own appearance according to its own liking. The closest Americans come to having a national costume is the baseball cap and the oversized T-shirt. They wear flip-flops to a dinner party or go to the theater in their tank tops and shorts. Schools announce a "Pajama Day" from time to time, and tousled-haired children show up in class in their footies. A college student will attend a professor's lecture in a sweatshirt and a pair of denims. Some CEOs wear hoodies to work and encourage jeans and sneakers, at the very least on Casual Fridays. Politicians, vying for the affection of the electorate, emulate the comfort-loving public and go tieless to convey ease and intimacy. That is why these presidential candidates like to be known by their one-syllable nicknames and show themselves in their jogging outfits and sneakers, running or shooting hoops. They do not just stride through barricaded walkways waving at crowds or shake hands with dignitaries. They get down and dirty, bowl at the bowling alley, flip pancakes at greasy diner flat tops. If they want votes, they must exude an easygoing spirit, so their constituents think them friendly enough to take along to the local pub.

ON SQUIRRELS AND AMERICANS

You used to give a coin or two to the poor of your city, or drop a banknote in the collection box at your place of worship, or help a neighbor or a friend with a loan. But these were a few small exercises at best. Here, people give regularly. Squirrels collect acorns, and Americans raise money. It is as natural as any instinct for them. Children offer lemonade on sidewalks to raise money for the kittens at the animal shelter. Girl Scouts go door-to-door selling cookies so other aspiring girls can become Scouts too, and do the same. Mothers organize bake sales to help pay for a new neighborhood playground. Teens give to the GoFundMe campaign of a filmmaker working on a documentary about the endangered aardvarks of Angola. Even Santa, the nation's gift giver in chief, appears at the threshold of major department stores every December, ringing a bell at the side of a siren-red donation bucket. Overworked cashiers will not scan your items before listlessly asking if you would like to donate a dollar to the fight against something or other. Once a year, arsonists take a day off so firefighters can stand at intersections holding up their rubber boots, charming drivers into pitching in a few dollars. At the registers of greasy gas stations, two things are always guaranteed: the noxious smell of fuel and the cardboard quarter receptacle for St. Jude Children's Research Hospital. In some movie theaters, films cannot start unless the ushers have walked aisle to aisle passing the empty popcorn container to collect money for whatever the star in the public service announcement urged the viewers to donate to. Entertainers hold telethons to raise money for this disease or that. Rock bands compose songs for disaster victims and give them their proceeds. Radio broadcasts are interrupted so the hosts can make appeals for a donation, which the local attorney or dermatologist matches. Runners run, bikers bike, and comics crack jokes, all to help raise money for the needy. Politicians bombard their supporters with emails, asking them to give five, ten, twenty, or more dollars toward making *a better tomorrow,* when, in addition to a higher minimum wage and universal healthcare, there will also surely be more emails asking you to donate again. Corporations have charitable arms. Dignitaries ask for money to build homes for the destitute. In television commercials, celebrities, holding doe-eyed babies in their arms, urge viewers to adopt a child on another continent through a monthly contribution. Anything is possible in America, even raising a baby by subscription.

When Americans do not raise money, they raise necessities. They have book drives, blood drives, food drives, turkey drives, even car drives. If they cannot solicit you in person, they send you letters. Heaps of envelopes arrive in America's mailboxes every week asking the citizens to donate to one organization or another. Fundraising is a behemoth as vast as any industry. There is even a day on the calendar dedicated to it. Black Fridays are to shoppers what Giving Tuesdays are to donors. You may be naturalized already, but unless you begin writing checks for people you have never met, living in places you would never visit, you are not a real American.

No nation so rich has ever asked for more money. They do not need the order or the permission of some authority to tell them what to raise and for what cause. They take matters into their own hands and wage campaigns to save the pandas, protect the bees, or reverse beach erosion. What is at the heart of all this fundraising is the same thing that is at the heart of all other perfectly American things—an irrepressible self. Fundraising is how the self asserts itself, and self-assertion is the first step on the road to self-invention. A single person is enough to start a toy drive for children in a war-torn country. Overnight, giant cartons appear at storefronts and in the lobbies of public buildings, and within days they are brimming with goods. Fundraising, and performing service in general, leave Americans believing that they are mightier than they really are. And what a boost it is to one's self-esteem to think that one is better off than others and in a position to lend a hand. The underlying sentiment, albeit a cliché, is to "make a difference in the world." However you feel about that ambition, you cannot deny that seeing them assume such a role, take the lead, and forge ahead, is positively stirring.

In certain circles, it is particularly chic to give. Donors name buildings after themselves, hoping to become slightly immortal with every brick. In suits, full haberdashery, and hard hats to boot, they lift a shovelful of dirt or pose beside a strip of ribbon with a giant pair of scissors alongside the governor, flashing their toothiest grins. They hold galas in magnificent ballrooms with every dinner plate worth hundreds or more. They raise and raise. They cannot help themselves. Sometimes they raise even after they have raised what they had set out to raise. Fundraising for a worthy cause is a fine deed. But in a grand hall where a gown-and-tuxedo-wearing crowd mill about, and the hammering countdown of the auctioneer knocks at every ear, fundraising for any cause takes on the trappings of a sport, its purpose mostly forgotten. At the end, the total sum donated becomes a measure of social clout. Americans have a way of overdoing things. They can enlarge a small, endearing act to such ungodly proportions that the soul slips from it, leaving only a spectacle behind.

These spectacles are as much about the sheer display of power as the cause for which they are staged. The charitable hosts know the price of that power, and of needing to do their part to prove worthy of it. They set high goals for, and expect a great deal of, themselves. They might apologize if they do not know the capital of your birth country, or pause over your name and admit that they cannot pronounce it. This they will say in a sheepish tone, as if embarrassed by their inability to enunciate every exotic sound in every tongue. They readily blame their government for much that is wrong in the world. When you hear this, you will likely think—but will say nothing—that they assume themselves masters of a universe in which there are no other factors or actors wielding influence but America. Among this elite, being critical of America is not an opinion. It is faith. This kind of self-deprecation may be mistaken for modesty. But it is, in fact, a disguise for narcissism, for it places America at the center of all events, where her mere intervention, however brief, can forever alter a nation's destiny. They lament and lament, and some will go as far as threatening to move to Canada, though the closest they ever get is to Niagara Falls, and even then, for only a weekend.

Do not think yourself immune. You will nurse your own

flawed views of America, just as everyone else. You will be tempted to make sweeping judgments about Americans after a few early observations. Only remember that they would not be the purveyors of universal dreams—in film, song, fashion, and literature to everyone, everywhere—if they were so simple to know. Quick declarations are easy to come by. Resist the urge! A few clichés or early impressions are not enough to know the heart of a nation. You spot a few obese bodies and pronounce everyone fat. You talk to someone who has never heard of your country and conclude that all Americans are ignorant and know nothing about the rest of the world. (Here, you would be wise to remember that you, yourself, know little about the far-flung others and cannot name the capital of Kyrgyzstan, or the prime minister of Holland, or the currency of Ukraine. You see, modesty is a virtue, sometimes even in America.) You watch them splitting the bill after a dinner and decide they do not know what friendship is. You look at the map of the nation divided into red and blue on election night and assume all of their politics is a mere binary matter of Democrat or Republican.

Even as Americans are the most observed and studied nation of all, they remain equally misunderstood. Everything is expected of them at all times, including things that are contradictory. They meddle in the affairs of other nations and are rightly criticized for it. But when a war breaks out and they do not intervene, they are criticized for being cruel and self-interested isolationists. When their volunteers go to the distant corners of the world to help others, their work is touted only within their own community. Their military lays down water pipes, builds homes, wires towns for electricity, trains locals in all manner of security and governance, and provides relief, especially at times of natural disaster. But all anyone ever hears of is the wars they wage. Americans are master marketers, yet the products they cannot seem to promote are their own good deeds.

Sorting truths from falsehoods about America is what you must do to fashion your own brand of American. Making sense of them on one hand, and making something of yourself on the other, are your foremost tasks. Once you had to free yourself from the burden of violence, poverty, discrimination. Now you are under the burden of expectation of success and gratitude. You cannot simply have come to America to be, you must become great, greater than their own average citizens, so that your champions can spin your life story into a good yarn for the cocktail hour. To succeed hinges, in great part, upon your ability to "Americanize." But it can either seem too abstract, or too daunting, for it might feel as though you must undo who you already are. Think of Americanizing not as a coat of paint to pour over all your existing hues but as an extra shade to artfully blend in with the rest. In other words, unless your own values clash with those of this culture—such as not believing in the equality of women with men, or in ethnic and religious coexistence—you do not need to subtract anything from who you are, only add to it.

THE THANKS YOU OWE

Surely learning the language, understanding the culture, embracing America's founding principles ought to be sufficient steps toward becoming an American. Yet the history of African Americans shows that none guarantee you will be recognized as an equal by your fellow Americans. If the measure of Americanness is in the perfect use of English, African Americans mastered the language, and some of their writers and orators have outshone the rest in eloquence. If the measure is in embracing the culture, they have gone beyond to invent much of the culture itself. If the measure is in sharing the faith of the majority, they have worshipped more fervently than their fellow faithful. If the measure is loving the country, they have fought and died in America's wars. Time and again, they have out-Americaned their fellow Americans. And yet, centuries since their tragic arrival, the wicked legacy of injustice and inequality still marks this nation.

Now that the discussion has turned to the darker aspects of the people to whose flag you will be swearing allegiance, it is time for you to know the ignoble truths about America, too. You must know that her economic supremacy has not come through ingenuity and natural riches alone. The Founding Fathers achieved what they did because the founding slaves were there to sweat and bleed to make their dreams come true. After all, it is easy to dream when you have armies of free laborers to make your vision a reality.

This is not a past without any bearing on you. Your fears and mistreatments share an ancestry with this heinous history.

If you are tolerated today, however reluctantly, it is because the slaves and their descendants forced tolerance upon this nation in spite of itself. Whether you are aware of them, or can trace the lineage of your presence to them and their suffering, you must know that their struggle for their rightful place has lessened your burden to struggle for your rightful place. American democracy began as an imperfect ideal. Every battle against its flaws perfected it a little more, and the hardest of those battles have been and continue to be fought by African Americans.

You can admire the movie stars and sports or music icons all you want, but the people who have truly made America face its own bigotry and confront its intolerance toward others are African Americans. You are the beneficiary of a long-standing struggle you were not a part of by people not your own. Democracy, as in "all men are created equal," was only a handful of pretty lines in gold-embossed books. It was the many decades of African Americans resisting, protesting, boycotting, bleeding, and languishing in prison that created the social laboratory in which those ideas were tested and made more true. In time you, too, must continue their fight to make this democracy more perfect by demanding to be seen, heard, treated as equal, or simply by standing with others who are doing so. It may have been a war that you ran away from to take shelter in America. But your fighting days cannot be over. There is no military draft here: some choose to become soldiers and fight on behalf of the country, and others do not. For the immigrant, a draft of a different sort is mandatory. You must fight on behalf of that original dream, to enlarge America's capacity to include new multitudes. You are here to fight for your place, which means for the values that make up the essence of this country. Americanism is a matter of mind and heart, said President Franklin Delano Roosevelt; it is not, and never was, a matter of race or ancestry. You must do all you can to tell the story of the slaves and their indispensable legacy to your children, because if their story fades, the story of immigrants will fade, too. Then, before you know it, you will no longer be welcome.

WHAT NOT TO LEARN FROM AMERICANS

Your old fears of gangs or guards will slowly abate. Beware not to fill those empty spaces with new evil. Once your enemies were men in clerical garb, thugs brandishing their weapons roaming the streets, plainclothed agents secretly watching your every move. No longer. Suddenly, your world may seem empty. You have lived with an enemy for so long that you may be at a loss without it. Beware not to adopt America's hostilities or unkind ways to fill the vacuum and create a sense of belonging. If you come from a culture that held its elders in high esteem, say the Philippines, you ought not commit your grandparent to a nursing home to show that you have assimilated. If you are fair-skinned, you do not need to exercise bias against the darker kind to prove that you belong here. If you are dark-skinned, say a Nigerian, you may feel frustrated by all those who impose upon you a history of discrimination that you have never been part of. Your skin color may not have been something you gave much thought to before, but suddenly another people's history is thrust upon you, and you find yourself preoccupied with anxieties you never had. Feel free to reject the ways others choose to shape and define you through their preconceptions.

Living here will now present you with an opportunity you could never have before. You can get to know the boogeymen of your past—the neighbor of a religion you had been taught to hate, or the colleague of another ethnicity, whom you were raised to believe were evil or lesser than you. Unlike in your homeland, you are not segregated from one another. Those whom you had avoided in the past circulate in your community just like the rest. America is the great equalizer. The ready access to all the people and spaces that were once beyond your reach will sometimes be to your advantage and sometimes to your disadvantage. For instance, if you are from Pakistan, you may find that you can shop nowhere else but at an Indian market, which carries the exotic spices and fruits other markets do not. Rolling your cart through the aisles of the Delhi Bazaar is a strange experience you can hardly describe to your relatives in Lahore. Every time you fill your bag with groceries, talk to Mr. and Mrs. Patel at the register, you leave with a little less dread of Hindus.

If you are Iranian, you will be flabbergasted when, dangerously short of breath one day, you are wheeled into the emergency room of your local hospital, where a Saudi American cardiologist will resuscitate you. As the air flows into your lungs again, you vow to thank any random Arab who crosses your path for the rest of your days. On Tuesday nights, when you walk into your Economics 101 class taught by a Rwandan teaching assistant, you no longer wonder whether her family was of Hutu or Tutsi origin. The laws of the markets, surplus, inflation, and supply and demand get in the way of the divisive curiosities you exercised long ago.

You may have already lived here for a few years, and yet America continues to enamor you in endless ways, except in one. Her satellites go deeper into the galaxy and find new celestial bodies to orbit. Just as you begin to look heavenward and exult in the discovery of a new planet, the news of another mass shooting breaks, and the electric feeling that had nearly lifted your spirit simply singes it instead. It is hard to celebrate the genius of any invention, or the cure for any rare disease, when more die of the bad laws that have armed the nation; impossible to boast of the might of the world's most advanced military while more Americans die at the hands of their compatriots at home than at the hands of their enemies abroad. Horrible things happened in your former homeland. Dissidents disappeared. Journalists were butchered. Girls were married off to ancient men. One ethnic group rose up against the other. Yet one thing never happened: no ordinary citizen, lawfully carrying an advanced automatic rifle, ever walked into a school and opened fire on children. All the achievements of an exceptional nation lose their glory in light of such brutality. Yet the right to own guns must remain intact, among other reasons, so hunters can hunt, even if their most common prey lately has been children. However destitute you may be upon your arrival, you can take comfort in that, unless there was a war, your children did not go to school fearing a massacre by their neighbors. They may not have had proper books, or benches, but their teachers did not have to train themselves to be ready for a battle against the fully armed madman who might break into their classroom. Americans may call you a "spick," "sand nigger," "towel head," "banana," or "wetback" to demean you. Yet none of these can ever be as offensive as this sanctioned savagery.

THE UNDOING OF AMERICA

Long ago, you came to America on a visa that has since expired, or you snuck in through the southern border. Whether you came by choice or by the force of circumstance, you probably, like all happy and unhappy newly arrived immigrants, experienced yourself as anomalous at first. Yet even among the anomalous, the undocumented are an exception. An arrival is usually about renewal, a second chance at opportunities that one never had. Not yours. Yours was about knowingly entering the new world as a lesser human. Others come here to dream. You had to bury your dreams. Arriving here as you did, with hardly any belongings, perfectly captured your new status. You could not afford the satisfaction of carrying a suitcase, of bringing along a few beloved objects, of being seen by the neighbors as a newcomer, and of having the burden of your loss known to others around you. You likely came with only a bag of dried beans, tortillas, cash for sundries and the smugglers, and a change of dark-colored clothing to keep you from standing out at the crossing. You rode one bus—at capacity with passengers and anxiety—then another and another through day and night.

When you got off, you remained jittery, still feeling the bumps of the rough, unpaved roads, and your stomach churned with motion sickness.

Like all maps, the map of America, too, stretches to four corners. But for you, every one of them pointed only to danger: north for heatstroke, south for scorpions and rattlesnakes, east for crooked human coyotes and traffickers, and west for the border patrol and self-appointed vigilantes. To deter snakes, you rubbed garlic on your shoes, lay still in the desert for so long that the sand's imprint blended with the scars on your skin. Lizards crawled up and nested under your sleeve. Blisters swelled large and angry on your feet.

You came to do the work the locals do not want, to turn yourself into a human dough to be shaped by an employer's design. The apartment you eventually found was not a home. It was only a place to crash. You came to work and send money to your family. Your kitchen was not a place to prepare a meal. It was where you gorged yourself on anything you could find before your shift starts again. A television was not there for entertainment. It was what you stared into to interrupt the images that your mind kept returning to over and over, so you could hypnotize yourself into sleep. And your bed . . . what bed? You got only a mattress on the floor, laid next to several other people like you were in a makeshift infirmary. At the end of every day, all you could do was rest long enough to do the same thing again the next day. There are rumors about you having come here to rape and rob. Given your workload, rape and robbery have to wait.

You live in poverty, and yet American poverty is no poverty compared to the one you escaped. If you are a mother, you have entrusted your kids to a relative and are childless now. In your children's minds, America is worse than divorce. It is where parents go to never return. It is the whale that swallows mothers and fathers and spits out a few packages of fancy denim and brand-name sneakers every couple of months in return. Meantime, you work seven days a week, yet you lurk around the edges of wherever you happen to be like a trespasser. You, the busiest worker in the neighborhood, become the person everyone uses but pretends not to need.

Or you might not even remember the crossing, or the life that came before it. It happened so long ago, or you were so young. For all that has faded from your memory, one wish has become vivid and irrepressible with the passing of years. Some families dream of a grand home, others a luxury car, an exotic vacation, or good health. Your family dreams of papers. In your household, papers do not represent mere pages to write lines or print images upon. Papers are what separate the lawful from the unlawful, the full human from the half human. You talk, think, and scheme about papers more than anything else. When they teach you about good nutrition and show you the diagram of a balanced diet, you think that the Food and Drug Administration forgot to leave a slice on that healthful plate for papers. Fruits, grains, and proteins are hard to come by without papers, and when they are available, the anxiety of not having papers can get in the way of consuming the wholesome items. You also have a thing or two to say to the sociologists

about their poor design of the pyramid representing the hier-
archy of needs. They accounted for all sorts of sustenance, but
not papers. Yet how much meaning can food and shelter afford
a life, especially in the long run, without papers? Papers are for
humans what wings are for birds: they let the bird do what a
bird is meant to—take flight and soar.

There are many misconceptions among Americans with
papers about those without. Some believe that America can
accept more refugees and immigrants and do what she has done
through the years—be a destination for people who have been
turned away. Indeed, America can, and should. Yet no matter
how many refugees she accepts, it will do little for the great
masses who are already on the move around the world, and the
many more who soon will be. No, America is not running out
of space, and she surely is not "full." Yet America cannot alone
solve the problem of the current or forthcoming refugees; no
single country or continent can. Nations must come together
to affect the forces that are causing displacement at their root.

Meantime, you are here, and have been for as long as you
remember. Every time someone says, "Go back to your country,"
you think hard to reach into your memory for the earliest place
you ever knew, and the effort takes you only to a neighborhood
in America. Even if you remember the old country, you no longer have any attachments to it. This is all the country you know
now. You never wished to be a magician, or to be an object in
a magician's hands. Yet there are moments when your life here
resembles a magic act. The traces of your presence are everywhere, but you are, and must do your best to remain, invisible.

You care for the ailing parents no one can or wishes to visit. You pick the fetching strawberries that will beckon under the misty glow of the fruit aisles. You are the reason the suburban shrubs are so meticulously shaped, the lawns of the golf courses so perfectly manicured. You add the scent to the folded garments in the dresser of the boss you have never met, who leaves a key for you under the doormat and an envelope of cash on the kitchen counter every Wednesday morning. You are why the trash cans in the offices are empty in the mornings and the drywall in the basements stands upright. Just like the magician's audience— who know that no woman can ever live through being sawed in half, yet suspend disbelief to enjoy the show—Americans, too, enjoy the taste of their berries, the look of their lawns, the comforts of their clean offices, not wondering how they got to be that way. When you leave home in the morning, no one knows for sure if you will return at the day's end. When you do, your family's suspense ends. If you do not return, there will be no awed crowds to applaud your artful disappearance, only ICE officers searching your apartment.

Everyone else walks on pavement. You walk as if on ice, no matter the season. For you, danger lurks everywhere. Others leisurely saunter the sidewalks, licking their ice cream, speaking loudly on their mobile phones. Not you. You hesitate to draw attention to yourself. People think you are shy or dumb. You are neither, only permanently scared. Even when the president signs an amnesty bill and invites all the undocumented to apply for residency status, you are too afraid to come forward. If there is a fight in your building, you cannot call for help. Most others turn to the police when there is trouble. Not you. You avoid them. Other drivers simply drive. You drive as if you are forever taking a driving test, seated beside an imaginary officer, fully alert and unnerved. You stare at the speedometer to make sure you stay under the speed limit. You always put your blinkers on when changing lanes and think twice about turning right on red, even where it is allowed. Your car is a wreck, but its mirrors are never cracked, its headlights always light up, and its registration and inspection stickers are never expired. You never drive with the top down, or blast music from your speakers. You have so rarely honked that you cannot remember the sound of your own car horn. This is how you have devolved from a human into a human mouse.

Life in America has disfigured you. When feet are bound, they are likely to get infected and become fetid. The person with bound feet will forever have an unsteady gait. If the whole human is bound, in your case by your circumstances, he goes about timidly. To stand tall, a person requires strong muscles and bones, but also confidence—in the self and the possibilities ahead. If you cannot know what tomorrow will bring, there is nothing any muscle or bone can do to make up for the ungainliness of uncertainty.

The disfigurement does not end with you. The employer who hires you but does not give you a raise or benefits, the family that slips you cash and never pays you overtime, the supervisor who molests you—all of them knowing that you can have no recourse—through these inhuman practices, they have become disfigured, too. Even as a parent, you are disfigured. You are mostly the façade of a parent, because you cannot give your children what they most need—above all a sense of security that you will always be there for them. The truth is that you are a ghost and can vanish at any moment. You cannot console them, because you are despondent yourself. You cannot teach them to be brave, because you are filled with fear. If and when you are finally deported, no one will send your children flowers or offer condolences. There are no funerals for ghosts. If you or your life are an example to your children, it is only the example of the life they should do their best to avoid.

In time, your children will be similarly disfigured. They will go to school but soon find that learning will do nothing to change their lot in life and will see little reason to learn. Disfigured students will, in turn, disfigure the school, which cannot do what a school is meant to do: cultivate the hope that education can lead them out of misery. Your children will become disillusioned, and nowhere but in disillusionment can depression, poverty, or violence find better breathing ground. When this goes on for long enough, you will make America's worst fears come true: you will not learn English, or embrace this culture, or identify as American. Why would you learn English? How will English improve a life that has no shot at the future? Everyone else can get ahead. Not you. You have nowhere to go. Learning is for other people. Not you. If America will not have you, you will not insist. You will not have America either. And this is how the land of immigrants, the nation that has boasted of seamlessly blending all groups into one people, will cease to be what it has always been.

Sooner or later, your neighborhood will be disfigured, too. You do not trust the local police or authorities. You do not know the mayor or the town representatives—why should you?—and while you abide by the laws because you are afraid of them, you do not believe in their fairness. Since you do not have the privileges of a citizen, you do not feel obligated to perform the responsibilities of a citizen, even if you knew them. What neighborhood can ever thrive if it is populated by hopeless people who have no incentive to participate in the life of their community? Then your town, later your city . . . eventually America herself is disfigured, because her democracy has not done what it pledges. Hundreds of thousands of her residents have sorry lives, little liberty, and no way to pursue happiness, though they carry on cleaning, pruning, painting, caretaking, and babysitting for everyone all along. In the end, you become the fine print at the bottom of the American contract, the human disclaimer to her democratic promise. For an example of how you might detect the presence of an undocumented person in your life, see Box 5.

BOX 5

The Unauthorized Biography of an American Asparagus

From a strictly botanical perspective, the asparagus is simply a plant of the lily family with branched stems and feathery foliage. Its name, from the Greek spargan, *means "to swell," which itself originates from the Persian* asparag, *"to sprout." It acts as a diuretic and is otherwise an excellent source of calcium, magnesium, and zinc and has a considerable supply of dietary fiber, protein, beta-carotene, vitamins B_6, C, E, K, and other minerals.*

From the pickers' perspective, however, these descriptions are deceptive, for they say nothing of what the mighty stalk does to them. Against this human backdrop,

the asparagus—wholesome by nature—becomes wholly harmful to its caretakers.
A look at the conditions of the vegetable and the picker reveals surprising parallels.
The asparagus are planted in beds, only two or more inches apart from one
another. Their pickers' quarters are similarly congested. Some live, a dozen or more,
in tiny apartments. (Note the asparagus's advantage here: while it is equally
crowded by fellow stalks, it does not need the proverbial personal space.)

After the harvest, the asparagus eventually returns, for it is a perennial plant.
The pickers, too, would do the same—go home to return for another harvest. In
fact, they were once happily seasonal: went back to Mexico, where the majority of
them come from, and returned in March, ready for the new crop. Nowadays, alas,
they cannot. The pickers, most of them undocumented, do not chance returning. The
price of a crossing has risen to two thousand dollars or more—an amount slightly
less than half of a season's pay. So they stay, biding their time, sending home their
pay or saving for a house in the family village, or the bride money for a wedding.

One great challenge to growing asparagus is weeds, which can easily besiege
the stalk and squeeze it dry. The pickers, too, undesirable outside the farm, can be
seized by threats of their own. Border agents, ICE officers, and local vigilantes
readily arrest and deport Mexicans, ending their livelihoods. However, in periods
of great disaster, like a pandemic, the agents look the other way, since, being
essential, the "outlaws" are suddenly called essential workers and become the
nation's chief suppliers of food at a time of scarcity.

The asparagus is highly useful in what is called "companion planting," as
it helps keep off some of the pests that harm the tomato plant, among other
vegetables. But what the asparagus can do for the tomato, it cannot do for its
human caretaker. It cannot guard against the evils that come to them, for instance,
lessen the berating they suffer by their superiors. They work an average of fourteen
hours per day between March and May, where a typical day passes as follows:
Rise before dawn. Wash face. Avoid drinking coffee (for there will be no bathroom
breaks on the farm). Punch in. Pick a row. Walk to the first spear. Measure to see if
it is nine inches long. If so, bend and stab the stalk with the long-armed asparagus
knife and drop it in the bucket at your waist. Walk to the next spear, repeat. If you
rest or slow down, you will lose time, and your pay will follow suit.

It is fortuitous that the perfect soil for the asparagus is a maritime one, rich
with saline, for the laborers are sure to add to the brine with their sweat and tears.
Fortunately for the consumers, the suffering that the cultivation of the asparagus
inflicts does not get passed on. Therefore, the nutritionally watchful and morally
conscientious American citizens, who prefer to eat vegetables to improve their own

health or lessen the cruelty toward domesticated creatures, remain unaware of the cruelty their green diet inflicts upon their fellow humans.

At the day's end, the asparagus emerges from the sorting lines and conveyer belts rinsed, bundled, boxed, cooled, and then is loaded onto trucks. The pickers go to a meal that has no trace of the fresh greens they pick all day—often a hamburger and fries at the local burger joint. And such are the third-world conditions under which the greatest global superpower arrives at most of its homegrown vegetables.

E AS IN ÉMIGRÉ, AS IN
EXCELLENCE

As the years go by and you feel more at home here, the deeper questions begin to loom. You wonder how you can become the American you do wish to be. Since the self and its rights got their start in this country, it is most fitting that you, too, begin at those origins. Only for you, the path to "life, liberty, and the pursuit of happiness" passes through the pursuit of excellence. To some, excellence may be more synonymous with gaining wealth. You, too, may dream of being rich. Whatever your wish, it is wisest to get to it through hard work and personal achievement. For instance, if you decide to open a restaurant, you ought not simply be satisfied with cooking. You must aim to become a superb chef. If you choose to join a swim team, you cannot only come to the meets; you must learn to glide in water as fast as the fish. You cannot just spell; you must place first in the National Spelling Bee. Arriving in America, however herculean an effort it took, was only half of the ultimate feat. Belonging is the other. Excellence is the surest way to belonging.

If the job you perform brings little pay, you may feel unsure of yourself and your own significance. Here are a few questions you can ask to remind yourself of your value when others dismiss and overlook you: Who but you would be willing to stand before the oven on unforgiving August days and bake pizzas for their children's birthdays? Who but you would care for the sick in their underserved communities? Who but you would move into the neighborhoods they have long abandoned and restore life to their blighted blocks? Who but you would be willing to wipe the bottoms of the demented parents who have forgotten their own children, and whose children wish they could forget them? What you earn may be small, yet the importance of what you do is infinite. That, too, is excellence.

Still, excellence may not always lead to the kind of success you hope for, despite your efforts and perseverance. In the field of hard sciences, being an immigrant may slow you down at first but not for long. Becoming a top doctor, mathematician, or researcher depends far more on your mastery of the universal scientific language than anything else. In pursuing a career in the arts or literature, on the other hand, your ambitions can easily turn into anxiety. A painter, a musician, a dancer can still shine. But being an actor onstage with your stubborn accent is nearly inconceivable. More inconceivable yet is becoming a writer. It took every bit of courage you could muster to simply live and work among Americans, but to write, too? You may have fallen in love with English, with its precision and audacious syntax, yet you cannot help but worry that having arrived at it as a second language forever makes you a second-rate writer. It is one thing to tread on their roads, another to tread on their language.

Before you decide against becoming a writer in America, ponder the idea for a while. The obstacles are already clear, but the advantages are less so. For you, sentences can become the filaments with which to weave a new cocoon. The search for a home will be your perennial quest. No matter where you go, you will always be looking for it. Consider the white serenity of the page. You might find that it can be a haven in its own right. Why think of home as a physical place at all? Words can be the bricks to a trustier home in the mind.

The stresses that may burden other writers are unlikely to bear on you. What have you to prove at all now that you have survived your crossing into America? No achievement will ever surpass your coming to this country. From the safety she grants you, you can bear witness more than you ever have. On the page, you can remake what is lost. There the life that was torn away can be pieced together with the present. What have you got to lose? The anxieties that dog your fellow native-born writers will not be yours. For you, if a book turns out not to be a best seller, so be it. You will not despair. However well or poorly it is received, you will still be ahead. You will still be thrilled that you wrote what you thought you might never live to write, thought what did not get censored or cause you to get arrested, imprisoned, or executed. After all that, if you go on to be even published, well . . . as Americans say, that is just gravy!

EIGHT

On Refusing to Move
to the Back of the American Bus

The Utopia of imagination, is not the United States of our
experience. By substituting fancy for judgment, romantic
hopes are first formed to be afterwards destroyed.

—JOHN O'HANLON AND EDWARD J. MAGUIRE, *Reverend John
O'Hanlon's The Irish Emigrant's Guide for the United States* (1976)

You are afraid of the news lately. Every day in the headlines
much evil is leveled at the people of your ethnicity. When it
comes to popular sentiments about immigration, the bad news
is the same as the good: anti-immigrant hostilities are as old as
America herself. Take heart! Let them fight you! Someone else
had fought their ancestors, too. Someone else had humiliated
their great-grandparents for the look of their garb, the shape
of their caps, the smell of their food. Your community might
be the object of hate and suspicion today, but it will not remain
so forever, and with any luck, not even for long. While knowing this does not make living through these trying times any

easier, the notion ought to be comforting. Hating an immigrant community is America's hazing ritual. It means that a future generation, with undue adulation to make up for the spurns of their elders, will be ushering you into their fold.

Do not sulk or turn sour against your swarthy ancestry. The whitest of whites have been hated, too, indeed worse than you might be. Are the French, whose ways Americans now believe to be highly refined—their women most alluring, their cuisine superb—white enough in your view? They, too, were once rejected by America. President John Adams devised the Alien and Sedition Acts in 1798, which Alexander Hamilton, the founding immigrant, endorsed. The allegiance of French immigrants, labeled as members of a "hostile nation," came under suspicion because of an undeclared war between the United States and France. According to the new law, they could be deported, or even imprisoned. Do you think that the five-year process you must undergo to naturalize is excessively long? The authors of the Alien and Sedition Acts required immigrants to wait fourteen years before they could naturalize, which, given the longevity rates in the eighteenth century, was a slice of eternity in any applicant's lifetime.

Do not dwell upon the unfeeling lexicon of terms that are used to refer to you and your status. You work hard to blend in, yet it all turns into naught on a form, where you must check the box "resident alien." *Alien?* Crestfallen, you might conclude that no matter who you become and what you do, you will always remain a stranger on record. Another term that puzzles you is "naturalization." In your mind's anxious state you will brood over a logical question: Are you unnatural before you undergo the process? Are you assumed abnormal or malevolent in your pre-citizenship state? Will taking the Oath of Allegiance subsequently restore you to normalcy? You will surely find reasons to take offense at the term if you mull it over for long. Let it go. Better to reserve this kind of linguistic cross-examination for the crossword. But in case you cannot, taking a closer look at the word might prove reassuring. "Naturalization" has a stony feel, but its etymology is surprisingly supple:

naturalize (v.)

1550s, "admit (an alien) to rights of a citizen" (implied in naturalized*), from* natural *(adj.) in its etymological sense of "by birth" + -ize. In some instances from Middle French* naturaliser. *Of words or expressions, "adopt as native or vernacular," 1590s. Of plants or animals, "introduce and acclimatize in places or situations where they are not indigenous," by 1708.*

Naturalizing, you see, is about being introduced to a new place and acclimating, like replanting an unhappy shrub in friendlier earth, which in the farming economy of the eighteenth century was a respectable act. It is, nonetheless, ironic that the term "naturalize" should come from French, the language of the very people who, themselves, could not be naturalized in 1798. Who knows why or how these swings—banning an immigrant group in one era, revering them in another—happen in the American psyche. What is clear is that this psyche has an unusual propensity for extremes. It sometimes drives itself feverish, only to cool off and reconcile with the routine 98.6 again.

ANTI-IMMIGRANT VITRIOL
AS THE OTHER APPLE PIE

German immigrants did not have it any better. In the 1750s, another Founding Father, Benjamin Franklin, thought them lowlier than all the rest. Everything about Germans irked Franklin, no matter how small. He even loathed their street signs, in which both the German and English names were painted, and lamented, in a 1753 letter to the English botanist Peter Collinson, that the unassimilated German population in Pennsylvania were "generally of the most ignorant Stupid Sort of their own Nation." Do you think today's popular metaphor comparing immigrants to swarming pests is a new coinage? Or the fear that their invasive hordes will destroy the American way is unique to your time? Franklin, the founding inventor, thought of it first. He warned Collinson, "Unless the stream of their importation could be turned . . . [the Germans] will soon so out number us, that all the advantages we have will not . . . be able to preserve our language, and even our Government will become precarious." Franklin was, indeed, prejudiced. As America was beginning to chart its own path, he wished for British culture to be the model after which this nation shaped itself. But that was not the only reason he objected to the presence of German immigrants in his state. In a 1751 essay, "Observations Concerning the Increase of Mankind, Peopling of Countries, &c.," he confessed to being "partial to the Complexion of [his] Country" and brazenly said that certain people were simply unfit for America. Among the unfit, those of a "swarthy Complexion," he included the French, Russians, and Swedes.

Another Founding Father, John Jay, also the first chief justice of the Supreme Court, proposed erecting "a wall of brass around the country for the exclusion of Catholics" during the Fourth New York Provincial Congress in 1776. You see, America's history of discriminating against the outsider has been an indiscriminate one. Every race, every religion, even every class—no matter how powerful—has, at one point or another, been subjected to it.

Then there was the father of the Founding Fathers, George Washington, who dreamed of the America that has since drawn the dreamers of the world to her harbors. He once wrote to the Dutch Patriot minister Francis Adrian Van der Kemp, "I had always hoped that this land might become a safe & agreeable Asylum to the virtuous & persecuted part of mankind, to whatever nation they might belong . . . to settle themselves in comfort, freedom and ease in some corner of the vast regions of America." To Moses Seixas and his Hebrew congregation in Newport, Rhode Island, Washington divined a country where "every one shall sit in safety under his own vine and figtree, and there shall be none to make him afraid." He noted, "For happily the Government of the United States, which gives to bigotry no sanction, to persecution no assistance requires only that they who live under its protection should demean themselves as good citizens, in giving it on all occasions their effectual support." Everything about the vision of the visionary in chief was groundbreaking, except that it granted citizenship and protections from persecution only to white Americans. And so Washington could continue to be the master of his own 123 black slaves, until, at last, he set them free.

Bigoted notions might have begun with the leaders, but they did not end with them. Newly resettled immigrants were no kinder to those who came after them, not even to their own. America was a fortress to them. Each group that arrived wished to shut the gates to keep out the ones behind. They flocked here because it was the destination for anyone who needed shelter. Yet once they made their safe passage, they tried to remake it into an exclusive society. The British did not want the French, Russians, or Germans, and if they did, it was only as laborers to work their lands. The Italians did not want the Irish and the Irish did not want the Italians, and neither liked the Jews or African Americans. These days, Mexicans are as unwanted as the Chinese were a century ago, before the Chinese Exclusion Act was repealed. Back then, Mexicans freely crossed the border into the United States. That is why some Chinese who wanted to come to America traveled to Cuba or Mexico, learned a bit of Spanish, donned a poncho and sombrero, and entered disguised as Mexicans. A very absurd but recurring theme in the cycle of hate in this nation's history. Remember to resist such inclination in yourself. Do not reject others who wish to do what you have done and emigrate to America. To exclude them would not simply be wrong, but it would also undo the magic of America.

ALL MEN ARE CREATED EQUAL EXCEPT SOME MEN

You might wonder what America's educators and leading thinkers were doing to rid the nation of these exclusionary views. In a few but prominent instances, alas, they were working to advance them. Some of this country's greatest minds were generating or validating bigotry, disguising the ugliness of it behind highbrow data. Only a hundred years ago, at several storied Ivy League institutions, groups like the Race Betterment Foundation and American Eugenics Society had formed. The scholars who established these societies believed that there were, indeed, lesser people who had no place in America. Alarmed by the toll that World War I had taken on the young, they worried about the future of their own kind. The "chosen," their euphemism for white men, who had gone to fight the enemy abroad either had not returned or had returned but were having few offspring. This, in their opinion, was "race suicide," a term that President Theodore Roosevelt popularized to convey his concern for the decline of Anglo-Americanism.

Do not make the common mistake of thinking that it was, that it *is,* the uneducated or the disaffected who have harbored small-minded views. The sins of the elites are far greater. Their lofty language has a way of refurbishing every old malice into something fresh and respectable. In 1921, the renowned economist and first president of the American Eugenics Society, Irving Fisher, delivered a speech at the Cold Spring Harbor Laboratory. Instead of addressing the inequalities that were defacing America at the time, Fisher was proposing ways to save "the well-to-do classes" from being replaced by those who were "unintelligent, uneducated and inefficient." Fisher and other scholars who sympathized with his cause were not in their studies or laboratories trying to cure disease, eradicate poverty, or improve literacy. Instead, they were contemplating how best to "breed out the unfit and breed in the fit" so the white race could continue its dominance.

Were other prominent figures any kinder or more enlightened? Not if Samuel Gompers, the first president of the American Federation of Labor and its president for decades, was any example. He, who one expects would have cared about the plight of the underdog, stood against the struggling immigrant. Proposing a complete ban on employing Chinese immigrants as workers, Gompers wrote in a 1902 federation pamphlet, "The free immigration of Chinese would be for all purposes an invasion by Asiatic Barbarians. It is our inheritance to keep civilization pure and uncontaminated. We are trustees of mankind."

The simple truth is that throughout American history, the people who performed the hardest work this nation most needed were the most detested. The Native Americans who enabled the Pilgrims to survive their early days in the new country were later slaughtered by their descendants. The African Americans whose suffering fueled the engines of this economy lived as slaves, then under segregation until the 1960s. The Chinese who helped build large swaths of the Transcontinental Railroad, which transformed western America from a wild frontier into a web of commerce, lived as lesser citizens until 1943, when Congress finally repealed the Exclusion Act. The

Irish who built the Erie Canal, which changed the fortunes of the Northeast, were turned away by shop owners who displayed signs in their windows that read "Irish need not apply." The Italians, who gave America her beloved national food, the pizza, built the New York subway system, and manned the shores and the fisheries on the West Coast, were thought to be mobsters and treated as criminals. The Jews aboard ships escaping the Holocaust—the very people who cured polio and gave America her favorite attire, jeans—were sent back to their deaths in Europe, while Japanese Americans, who powered the farming and fishing industries, were placed in internment camps. In other words, Americans resist you until they no longer can. Your beloved bagels, burritos, biryanis, and bibimbaps break the monotony of their hot dogs and hamburgers, but they would prefer cooking them up without you. Every generation fights the influx of another ethnicity, until that ethnicity indelibly weaves its mark into the fabric of the community. Then they are treated as though they had always been there.

If your people are under a ban today, this might be a consolation: for nearly all of the twentieth century, no other country in the Western Hemisphere but the United States allowed their foreign-born residents to naturalize and become full citizens. Whatever her sins and flaws, America remains the pioneer, however imperfectly, in accepting immigrants. Even if you are treated as a suspect now, think of it as merely the same long-standing welcome America has given to others before you. Keep everything in perspective, or you will drown in self-pity.

And of all the things that could happen to an immigrant, self-pity is among the worst. It does what the nativists wish to do to you: convince you that you are too odd ever to fit in. They want to drive you out and back to the bosom of your ethnic or religious community, so they can go back to theirs and declare you unwilling to embrace America.

GIVE ME YOUR POOR VS. YOUR FAT CATS

The Alien and Sedition Acts, the Chinese Exclusion Act, and other such old laws have given way to today's immigration quotas and bans on various nationalities. But prejudice does not need laws to manifest itself. Given a chance, it rears its head, no matter the era. These days, it presents itself as the sensible, practical, or even necessary course of action. It disguises itself in a popular argument: America can no longer afford to accept the tired, the poor, the huddled masses, only immigrants with exceptional abilities or great wealth.

Nothing would be a greater offense to George Washington's vision. He knew that the task of building a nation was not the same as putting on a pageant or building a float for a parade. Turning refugees away to exclusively cherry-pick among potential immigrants is not how America became America. Do not be intimidated by this talk of special qualities and think yourself inadequate. America has always opened its doors to professionals with special skills, and understandably so. Those who have "special abilities"—persons with unique skills or sizable bank accounts—may never be what *you* can be, or might already be: a believer in the American cause. The supremely talented and the rich make good patrons but not always devoted patriots. Their entry is based on a transaction. In exchange for their skills or wealth, they receive visas. From their perspective, America has done them no favors by allowing them in, since they come with their fortune in tow. So what is to hold them back if someday a more lucrative offer comes along? What vow, what debt will commit them to this country?

You were granted entry based on nothing but goodwill and the belief that even the uprooted deserve to see a second season. Someday, or perhaps already, your father, mother, or you will tell the story of your arrival: *We came with no English, only a few dollars, and no one to depend on. It was hard at first. Work was grueling, but look at us now . . .* This is the drama at the heart of the American identity. It is the story of beating the odds to rise from brokenness, if not rags, to comfort and possibly riches. This common tale so many share molds the immigrant into a patriot and bonds American to American.

Those who come here already rich and talented hardly have a place in this narrative. If they were admitted because they are top engineers in their fields, then they will go on to do the same or better here. If they were admitted because they are wealthy, they will perhaps grow wealthier yet. But that is not how the nation's bond is cemented. Instead, the tale that begins with someone—say, you—who once upon a time had been turned away from every place, except one, has all the signs of an inevitable love story. Who can but be loyal to the one who tended to him when he was at his lowest? It is how a stranger transforms into a citizen. The immigrant who arrives empty-handed, then finds peace and livelihood, enters into a covenant with the country that sheltered him when he most needed it.

However resilient you may be, you might still find it hard to withstand the hostile racket on the news. And yet, you must do just that in whatever way you can. If talking, reasoning, and brooding fail, you must overcome your anxiety by simply doing things to occupy your mind. If you have no hobbies, pick up crocheting, or plant a few blooming bushes in the yard to have something to fuss over. And if these do not appeal to you, try singing some hymns or incantations. The latter can be especially affirming. If their tune is familiar and their words fitting, such a song can be a lullaby and a battle cry at once. Adapt any song, the more patriotic the better, and fashion it in whatever way you wish, to reflect your own hopes and dreams. No one will inject you into the American story; you must do it yourself. Remember that the spacious skies and amber waves of grain and purple mountain majesties alone cannot make a country if there are no people who lovingly work to make it livable. The American mountains are grand, the nature dazzling. But beautiful land-scapes do not always make for happy nations. The people who envision just societies and those who work to build them do. You must not be silent. You must blare these truths in whatever way possible. You must create your own anthems, speaking of the majesty of your own presence. To help inspire your own renditions, see the following sample stanzas.

Americans the Beautiful

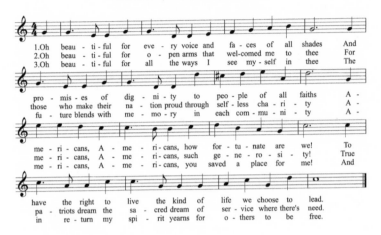

1.Oh beau - ti - ful for eve - ry voice and fa - ces of all shades And
2.Oh beau - ti - ful for o - pen arms that wel-comed me to thee For
3.Oh beau - ti - ful for all the ways I see my-self in thee The

pro - mis - es of dig - ni - ty to peo - ple of all faiths A -
those who make their na - tion proud through self-less cha - ri - ty A -
fu - ture blends with me - mo - ry in each com - mu - ni - ty A -

me - ri - cans, A - me - ri - cans, how for - tu - nate are we! To
me - ri - cans, A - me - ri - cans, such ge - ne - ro - si - ty! True
me - ri - cans, A - me - ri - cans, you saved a place for me! And

have the right to live the kind of life we choose to lead.
pa - triots dream the sa - cred dream of ser - vice where there's need.
in re - turn my spi - rit yearns for o - thers to be free.

AMERICA'S DARK FUTURE

Some of the mistreatment you experience has a long-standing history. Some is new, rooted in the foreboding of an unprecedented tide on the verge of turning. America's future is about to become darker than it has ever been. Dark not as in grim, but as in pigmented. The complexion of the nation will no longer be so white. By 2044, Caucasians will not make up the majority, and the order that has held for more than three hundred years will not hold anymore. Asians, the fastest growing immigrant group, will unseat the racial majority that has thus far steered this nation. Even though the fair-skinned prefer to appear sun-kissed—therefore the abundance of tanning sprays and salons—they are, nonetheless, intimidated by the imminent shift. This forecast has prompted fear rather than self-reflection. Those who had thought that belonging to America was simply a matter of the geographical accident of their birth or skin tone need to instead reexamine their beliefs, and ask, What ought to be the quality that makes an American?

The answer is simple: devotion to America's founding principles. If you believe that all people have the right to life, liberty, and the pursuit of happiness, that ideas and speech must be aired and protected, that people of diverse backgrounds can come together over the love of those values, that serving the country—through the army, unions, Rotary Club, volunteer groups—is the way to unite the people, that every person deserves a vote and equal regard before the law, then you are an American. Would the anxious Caucasians feel reassured to hear that though you do not share their skin tone, you do share these ideals? Perhaps not. But it is your duty to commit to these principles and pronounce them often. It is only a matter of time until everyone realizes that America, with its grand ambitions, can never belong to any single group, no more than paper can be Chinese, or penicillin British. Like all great discoveries, America, the modern world's first democratic invention, belongs to everyone. She is a mecca for all who dream her dreams. At a time when the towel on your rack is Turkish, the shirt on your back Vietnamese, the dinner on your plate Indian, the stock of purity cannot but plummet far. There is as much use for puritanism today as there is for horse-drawn buggies.

This is what the anxious native-born do not know, or have forgotten. They might blame you for the social or economic failings of their country. And you, being new, fear them. Yet it is *you*—so hungry for a fresh beginning—who are far more essential an ingredient in the American brew. This vast mix, made up of so many multitudes of people, is the reason for this nation's unrivaled edge. This is what you must remember, if you remember nothing else: even powerless, moneyless, and Englishless, you are the agent that this diversity needs to augment its prodigious ambition. Others who are enamored of America's financial wealth may not recognize how this nation's intellectual wealth came into being, and attribute her greatness to the former. Perhaps, in some divine or merely accidental way, you are here to remind them of their majestic inheritance and how it came to be.

There are drills you must master to best make your own case. You must learn to recount all the many ways in which you contribute to America, for instance: "Between 2005 and 2014, refugees and asylees [in the United States] from 1980 on contributed $63 billion more to government revenues than they used in public services." Will this sway the opinion of your detractors? Not likely. But it will affirm to you, if to no one else, that you and your brethren, however broken you might feel on the inside, renew this land as all those who came before you have done. When in doubt, decide against modesty in America. Have you seen the buildings and arenas the various benefactors name for themselves? You, too, are a benefactor to America. Broadcast to everyone how much you and your fellow immigrants, documented or not, pay in taxes, and how much safer you make your communities compared to those of the native-born. A great deal of what you do you do in anonymity, which is why you can be readily painted as dispensable. It is time to make yourself seen and heard. Silence will be the end of you. Do not lose sight of why you must do what you do; you may be unwelcome and unwanted, but you do not have to be unheard, too. Therefore, speak up and question those who question you. Ask for nothing other than their ears. Your enemies do their best to paint you as beastly. You must tell them your tale if you are to restore your own humanity.

In the meantime, know that you are not alone. You have allies, even if you do not know them. For all the bigots and eugenicists, there are also those who, however quirky or self-interested, will embrace and lift the immigrant.

THE MOST RELIABLE GODS

If the stress of these times is driving you to pray, then you might as well pray to the right deities, the most reliable patron saints of immigrants in America: (1) the Constitution, (2) Mother Nature, the Deliverer of Large-Scale Disasters, and (3) War and Other Man-Made Catastrophes. Below are three examples of divine intervention by these deities:

1. The Miracles of the American Constitution: In 1882, the Chinese Exclusion Act became the law. During the sixty years it was in effect, it prevented the Chinese from naturalizing, and for the first several years, even those who were born in the United States could not claim their birthright of citizenship. It barred Chinese immigrants from attending public schools and receiving care in hospitals, and some, like miners and fisher-

men, were subject to special taxes. Since they could not vote, they were of little interest to politicians, or even the local police, who offered them no protection.

Then one American-born Chinese man took an unusual step. In 1895, he went back to China on a brief visit. Upon his return, he was barred from re-entering the United States. He subsequently sued the State of California and the case went to the Supreme Court. Citing the Fourteenth Amendment, his attorneys argued that "all person[s] born or naturalized in the United States, and subject to the jurisdiction thereof, are citizens of the United States and of the State wherein they reside." They insisted that the word "persons" did not distinguish among ethnicities or religions and included everyone. The Supreme Court agreed. This victory changed the fortunes of many Chinese Americans, who were recognized as U.S. citizens thereafter. From then on, Chinese immigrants saw the Constitution as their best ally in their struggle for racial equality and filed dozens and dozens of lawsuits that chipped away at their exclusion.

2. The Miracles of Mother Nature's Disasters: The best example in this category is the great earthquake that shook San Francisco in 1906. The most powerful quake ever to hit the city, it claimed three thousand lives and turned many neighborhoods into piles of rubble. What the first shocks did not destroy, the fires they sparked

turned into ashes. The blaze reached Chinatown, too, and burned down most of it. But for the Chinese, the ash proved better than gold, and the quake a blessing. When the flames died and life resumed, many residents had lost their legal documents in the fire and had to apply for new government-issued identification and other certificates. The city's Chinese residents, some of whom had long wished to naturalize but were barred by the Chinese Exclusion Act, claimed to have lost their documents and applied for new ones along with everyone else. However, now they could falsify their birthplace on the new application and claim to have been born in the United States, which no one could deny or substantiate. The government had no choice but to issue new birth certificates for them. In the end, countless Chinese immigrants were able to become U.S. citizens and finally bring their wives and children to America.

3. The Miracles of Man-Made Catastrophes: Lastly, we come to the mixed blessings of man-made disasters, among which war is the chief example. Until the 1941 bombing of Pearl Harbor, the Chinese, subject to the Exclusion Act, had been treated as second-class citizens. But on the morning of December 8, 1941, their lot changed. Japan became America's greatest enemy, and Japanese Americans, suspected as traitors, were rounded up and sent to internment camps. Since those

who had to do the rounding up could not tell the Japanese from the Chinese, the government issued special buttons for the Chinese to pin on their lapels that read "Chinese American." In all the decades that the exclusion laws were in effect, the name "Chinese" had rarely been paired with "American." Within a few days, the war did for the Chinese what sixty years of the exclusion had not allowed: ushered them into the American community.

THE NINE CIRCLES OF THE VETTING PROCESS

You must now have no doubt that the hassles you are experiencing today have the same poisoned wellspring as those of long ago. The old fearmongers who portray immigrants as dangerous are inducting a new generation into their fold, pushing to bar new groups of immigrants from entering in the name of safety. The word "security" passes many lips these days. *Security,* you think to yourself, and seethe. Do your accusers even know of trials you had to endure before getting here, much less experienced them? The forms you filed, the scans and checkups you consented to, the fingers the officers squeezed in their unkind grips and pressed in ink. You must speak of the steps of your vetting process as readily as the multiplication table you rattled off in fourth grade. Among a myriad of other vital facts, the native-born do not know the grueling ordeal you went through before you arrived, which is why they are prone to believing that your presence makes the country unsafe.

In recounting the details of your vetting process, do not forget the importance of proper tone and verbal finesse. If you are already naturalized and confident of your status, you can show pluck and challenge the unknowing among them who have no inkling how much you were screened, poked, and prodded until you were allowed entry. But if you have yet to receive your green card, or are still waiting to take the Oath of Allegiance, you will want to exercise some Dale Carnegie diplomacy. In other words, try to "win friends and influence people" by putting your convictions to them as mere queries or suggestions. For instance, avoid saying, "You're not worth your salt if you believe that immigrants of any stripe pose a greater danger to the U.S. than the 280,000 to 520,000 bump stocks that are in circulation." Instead, you should knit your brow as if puzzled and present the idea as a question, remembering to always start with a "Hmm," so you appear to be contemplating the matter. "Hmm . . . I don't know the ways of this country nearly as well as you, which is why I'm hoping you could help me understand why the immigrants who undergo months of screening and background checks of multiple kinds are, in your esteemed view, a greater danger than the unlicensed businesses that are federally exempt from having to do a background check before selling a firearm?" Unctuous? If you heap enough praise on the addressee, he will hopefully be too disarmed to think so.

Few odysseys are as complex as your multitiered immigration screening. Even before it had begun, you had reason to throw your hands up and walk away, as you queued up against the walls of the American embassy and were sent home day after day because there were too many people ahead of you. The native-born who have never had to renew a visa or file an immigration application dread a visit to the Department of Motor Vehicles. If they had ever met an immigration official, or stood in line for an interview to have their paperwork reviewed, they would prostrate themselves at the feet of the DMV.

Hell has fewer circles than your security check. At every step, you wondered whether this trial was truly a security examination or a plot to undo your resolve by undermining your dignity. So grueling was it, so discouraging, that the native-born would file dozens of lawsuits against several agencies before they would ever agree to put themselves through it. It exposes one's personal history in the way that the X-ray, MRI, and DNA test combined expose the secrets of one's physiology. First, there are the biometric requirements—photos, fingerprints. Then comes a background check by the Department of State for a special screening through the Consular Lookout and Support System. That is followed by a Security Advisory Opinion, which is followed by an interagency check by the National Counterterrorism Center. Once an applicant passes these tests, he qualifies for another set of screenings by three additional government bodies: the FBI, Homeland Security, and the Department of Defense (Syrians must also undergo an additional Syrian Enhanced Review). At any of these steps, there might also be a Fraud Detection and National Security Directorate assessment. Once the background check is done, the foreground comes into view: you in the flesh. You will be put through a multipart medical screening. Often, it will end in you having to get a fresh round of vaccinations you have already had, but because you fled your country without your medical records, you will have to surrender to the governmental needle anyway. Then comes the final step, the in-person interviews at the U.S. consulate and the written testimonies. In page after page, interview after interview, you must retell the wrenching story of your departure. Then there will be a new set of forms with endless and often senseless questions. You can bet that there will be more forms from the immigration authorities just as reliably as you can bet that there will be rain from the sky.

YOUR STORY, YOUR PRAYER

Despite the threadbare circumstances of your arrival, you are likely to have a better chance at succeeding in the United States than some native-born. In certain parts of this country where old businesses have vanished and new ones have not replaced them, the native-born are forgotten by their own. Unlike you, they do not have a tale to tell themselves other than one of failure, betrayal, and hopelessness. Having made it to America gives you reason to be self-assured and to trust in your own abilities. You may come from an ancient heritage, with a rich civilization, but that past has no bearing on your present. It is too remote and beyond the reach of your imagination. What fuels your confidence is the story of your unlikely passage. You, who walked through the desert for days. You, who survived the disease-infested camps. You, who sat in solitary confinement for days on end and emerged sane. You, who were kidnapped by the rebels, put on drugs, turned into a child soldier, and yet landed in America and made yourself whole again. You, who fled the gangs. You, who crawled through the bushes, lay with the lizards, outwitted the coyotes, and withstood the unbearable sun. You, who flung yourself onto the dry shore before the Coast Guard could turn you away. It is this tale of your incredible crossing and survival that makes you feel invincible. Your nation's ancient glories do not give you confidence. The fact that you sill breathe does. Where can you not go, what can you not do, if you came away from all that hell intact? What can possibly happen that you have not already known? If the bombs, the kidnappers, the thugs, the guards did not kill or catch you, who can? You are a human phoenix. The sooner you see this, the faster you rise.

When you no longer have to parrot your story for immigration officials, you will tell it by choice and from the heart. This second telling is clearly not required of you. It is for others to learn of the feats you accomplished and sacrifices you made to come to the place where they were born. The story is what most others do not have, or have forgotten. And it is your story that fuses with the story of America. This is what those who want to change the laws to not accept the poor and the persecuted into this country do not understand. They do not know that every generation needs a fresh crop of immigrants to renew the original narrative of this nation's beginnings.

You traveled thousands of miles to get here, but the even longer journey was the one from the fourteen-year-old you once were to who you are now, and the arduous arc that took you, say, from the one who was taught to hate America to the one who took refuge in her and grew to be devoted to her. You want to fight for her, perhaps not for everything that she is today, but for the essential ideas she stands for. You do not believe in confessions. But you do believe in repentance. Loving America, having come to believe in her as you do, is your repentance.

A COVENANT IN RED, WHITE, AND BLUE

All that you have read thus far is not meant to alarm you, make you sad or happy, terrified or comforted—only to help you see and prepare for the new life before you. When you left your birth country, you fled an inheritance—one of war, poverty, corruption, or persecution. In America, you have not come to bliss, only an inheritance you can hope to shape on your own. At first, your survival depends on how quickly you learn the language, find a job, and learn to drive. In the long run, it will depend on how much grit you can muster in yourself. Think of America as a bus. Bullies, in the form of politicians or nativists, will tower over you and demand that you give up your seat. Summon the Rosa Parks within and do not budge. You are not here to shrink and sulk at the slurs and snubs. Fight for your place! It is what America undoubtedly wants you to do. If she did not, she would not put you through the rites and the ceremonies she does not put the native-born through. Just think of how they are pronounced citizens: a mother gives birth, the baby gets a birth certificate, which will be a record of his name, his parentage, and a few other details. To the native-born, citizenship is granted in the oblivion of infancy, through the accident of birth.

When you naturalize, nothing will be routine or forgettable. America will make sure that you know what she wants of you, and how seriously. To the immigrant, citizenship is granted at the end of an odyssey in a ceremony that, in summoning anxiety and requiring preparation, compares only to the greatest rites you undergo at other major occasions in your life. For the native-born, the easy arrival only means that America is their homeland. For you, who have gone through the ordeal of the journey and the years of waiting to naturalize, America cannot but be the promised land.

Like all American events, naturalization also begins with a mammoth form, some twenty-plus pages long. Then come the interviews, oral and written exams, and a ceremony. The ceremony is usually held at the most symbolic place of all—a courthouse, where the rule of law reigns. The person who will administer the oath is often a judge. The trappings of the courthouse are reminders of what you have come to and why. Local officials, decked out in their Sunday best, shed their long, bureaucratic expressions and appear genuinely joyous. Of all the tasks they must perform throughout the workweek, this is the one they look forward to the most. Speeches in hand, they take turns at the microphone to welcome the crowd into the American family. They will tell you to not give up the traditions of your old culture, only add them to your new American life. There will always be a story about how that official's grandparent or parent had come to America as an immigrant, and look, only a generation later, her children are now judges and other notable leaders. They thank you for choosing to become an American, and no one will say anything about how they resisted you and fought against letting you in.

The voice of the state representative in your ear may bring back echoes of the shouts of the angry anti-American mob in your former homeland. You were a schoolchild then, and had repeated the same chant. Yet here you are, ready to raise your right hand and swear your allegiance to the flag of the enemy of those bygone years. You may be seized by guilt or grief for turning your back on your own origins, or you may be brimming with feelings of gratitude and devotion. Most likely, all these emotions will be brewing inside you at once, as all occasions of great significance always stir so much within. You never thought you could be remade, but you stand today as a second draft of the person you once were. All that goes through your mind is this: when your own country left you out in the cold, another opened her doors to let you in.

Singers belt out the national anthem, and the crowd wipe their quiet tears away. Then, from his bench, the judge makes a final speech. Someone will administer the Oath of Allegiance, and you will repeat the words under these poignant circumstances. These are the sentences the native-born do not have to say, much less raise a hand to swear to them as an oath before so many witnesses, in unison with others who appear as weathered as you. There will be more pomp and circumstance, uniformed men carrying Old Glory to the call of a bugle—visions and sounds that will forever remain in your memory.

If holding your naturalization certificate in your own grip at last does not bring tears to your eyes, reading the congratulatory pages from the U.S. Citizenship and Immigration Services will. Beneath several paragraphs welcoming you into your new country, there will be two columns, one titled "Your Rights," the other "Your Responsibilities." Under the first column you will read that you have the right to express yourself; to worship as you wish; to a prompt, fair trial by jury; to vote in elections; to apply for government jobs or run for office; and, lastly, to pursue "life, liberty, and the pursuit of happiness."

Under the second column are your responsibilities: to "support and defend the Constitution; stay informed of the issues affecting your community; participate in the democratic process; respect and obey federal, state, and local laws; respect the rights, beliefs, and opinions of others; participate in your local community; pay income and other taxes honestly, and on time, to federal, state, and local authorities; serve on a jury when called upon; and defend the country if the need should arise." You press the certificate and all the other pages in your hand, and stagger out of the courthouse, intoxicated with disbelief. The strangers whom you had stood beside—and whom you had shaken hands, sung songs, and waved paper flags with—step out, too, equally wobbly. Nothing has changed since an hour ago, yet nothing feels the same either. You all linger on the steps of the courthouse, milling about aimless and giddy. The thought of you being given the duties you once dreamed of makes you somehow more grounded. You feel as light as the piece of paper in your hand, but also sturdier in step for the confidence it gives. You will not be so easily disregarded anymore.

America, thus, chooses *you*. Naturalization—the new marriage that came on the heels of a long, drawn-out divorce—is here. It was not you; it was that other: The certificate vindicates you. The certificate is proof that you were not permanently broken and deserved to belong again. You have been renewed, validated, and recycled back into society, to be visible among others once more. That is what America has always done. That is what America knows how to do. Do not mistake the certificate for a deed. You can only guard her grandeur, not claim it. Citizenship does not give you the ownership of this land. It only gives you the honor of her stewardship, the pride of upholding her principles, and of keeping her fire burning to warm all the generations to come.

Acknowledgments

In the beginning, there was only darkness—no agents, no book contracts, no editors. Then came Sandee Brawarsky, and there was light! She introduced me to Jonathan Segal, who introduced me to Zoë Pagnamenta. It was, indeed, a backward way of doing business, but backward proved best, as did each of these three, in their own splendid ways.

I am most grateful to my Super PAC: Owen Fiss, who listened to my vague ideas about this book early on and helped me think it through. Steve Luxenberg, my former editor and author of two fantastic books and dozens of recommendation letters on my behalf. Sam Gejdenson, who has believed in everything I ever wrote.

I was a fellow at the Wilson Center for International Scholars and the Hadassah-Brandeis Institute at Brandeis University. The residencies gave me time to research and stew over the earliest drafts of this book. I must also thank the refugee relief organization HIAS, formerly known as the Hebrew Immigrant Aid Society, for what they did for me and my parents and thousands of other refugees from around the world. This book went into production in the year 2020, when carrying on with life's most mundane tasks had become nearly impossible. The fact that it exists owes a great deal to the exceptional staff at Knopf: Erin Sellers kept everyone on task, the thoughtful Ellen Feldman made every sentence better than it was, and Soonyoung Kwon exercised her artistry, all as if it had been 2019.

Several friends helped with the various aspects of this work. The talented composer Max Heath helped me adapt "America the Beautiful." Corinne Blackmer plied me with relevant books and research materials, and Ramesh Mazhari was, as she has always been, steadfastly there, fortifying me. Along with millions of women in Iran and elsewhere, I am grateful to Masih Alinejad for her electrifying example, and I cherish the gift of her friendship.

Between my last book and this, I lost two indispensable Christophers, Hitchens and Stevens—the first to cancer, the second to terrorism. I miss them for all the reasons thousands of others do, but I miss them especially because they had always been my first and most generous readers. With this book and all that I will ever write, I pay homage to the brilliant lives they led.

As for my sons, Elia and Kian, I thank them for being dissatisfied when their mother lost sight of what she most loved to do and only fussed over them. No one pressed me as hard as they did, asking every day how much I had written. I hope this is worth their wait. My dearest friend, Debbie Harding, waited too, but quietly worried over all the many solitary hours I spent. May these pages be a relief to her. And to my fellow refugee and husband, Ramin, who always knew why we both had to write, and why we needed to build a home of our own.

Sources

ARTICLES

Ahmad, Sidrah. "I Was Pulled from Sex Ed Class, Did Not Learn About My Body and Was Abused." *The Star*, July 12, 2018.

Aviv, Rachel. "The Cost of Caring." *The New Yorker*, April 4, 2018.

Bauer, Mary. "Trump Is Lying About Immigrant Crime—and the Research Proves It." Southern Poverty Law Center, May 17, 2019.

Brooks, Arthur. "We Can Learn Much About the American Dream from Ex-offenders Who Turn Their Lives Around." *Dallas News*, April 30, 2018.

Brooks, Arthur C. "How Loneliness Is Tearing America Apart." *The New York Times*, November 23, 2018.

Buiano, Madeline, and Susan Ferriss. "Data Defies Trump's Claims That Refugees and Asylees Burden Taxpayers." The Center for Public Integrity, May 8, 2019.

Chen, David. "What Would You Like in Your Welcome Package? Immigrants Offer Tips for an Official Guide to America." *The New York Times*, July 4, 1998.

Coe, Cati. "What Is Love? The Materiality of Care in Ghanaian Transnational Families." *International Migration* 49, no. 6 (2011): 7–24.

Conniff, Richard. "God and White Men at Yale." *Yale Alumni Magazine*, June 2012.

Davis, Kenneth. "The Founding Immigrants." *The New York Times*, July 3, 2007.

de Sales, Raoul de Roussy. "Love in America." *The Atlantic*, May 1938.

Dinh, Khanh T., Barbara R. Sarason, and Irwin G. Sarason. "Parent-Child Relationships in Vietnamese Immigrant Families." *Journal of Family Psychology* 8, no. 4 (1994): 471–88.

Ferdowsi, Ali. "Hajj Sayyah," *Encyclopaedia Iranica*, XI/5, 556–60.

Fisher, Marc. "Behind Trump's 'Go Back' Demand: A Long History of Rejecting 'Different' Americans." *The Washington Post*, July 15, 2019.

Flagg, Anna. "Is There a Connection Between Undocumented Immigrants and Crime?" The Marshall Project, May 13, 2019.

Foer, Franklin. "How Trump Radicalized ICE." *The Atlantic*, August 6, 2018.

Halpern, Jake, and Michael Sloan. "Welcome to the New World." *The New York Times*, January 26, 2017.

Hannah-Jones, Nikole. "Our Democracy's Founding Ideals Were False When They Were Written. Black Americans Have Fought to Make Them True." *The New York Times Magazine*, August 14, 2019.

"Helping Immigrants Become New Americans: Communities Discuss the Issues." U.S. Citizenship and Immigration Services, 2015.

Hirschfeld Davis, Julie, and Somini Sengupta. "Trump Administration Rejects Study Showing Positive Impact of Refugees." *The New York Times*, September 18, 2017.

Huang, Frederick, and Salman Akhtar. "Immigrant Sex: The Transport of Affection and Sensuality Across Cultures." *The American Journal of Psychoanalysis* 65, no. 2 (June 2005): 179–88.

Kakutani, Michiko. "I Know What Incarceration Does to Families. It Happened to Mine." *The New York Times*, July 13, 2018.

Kamarck, Elaine, and Christine Stenglein. "How Many Undocumented Immigrants Are in the United States and Who Are They?" Brookings, November 12, 2019.

Khazan, Olga. "Why Americans Smile So Much." *The Atlantic*, June 1, 2017.

Law, Anna. "The Irish Roots of the Diversity Visa Lottery." *Politico,* November 1, 2017.

McCoy, Terrence. "How Does It Feel to Be White, Rural and in the Minority?" *The Washington Post,* July 30, 2018.

Nemtsov, Boris. "U.S. and Russia Revive Cold-War Game of Provocative Street Names." *The New York Times,* February 12, 2018.

Okrent, Daniel. "A Century Ago, America Built Another Kind of Wall." *The New York Times,* May 3, 2019.

Rampell, Catherine. "The 1930s were a dark period for immigration policies. There's one way today's could be worse." *The Washington Post,* July 23, 2019.

Rao, Sonia. "'What's Up with That White Voice?': The Tricky Art of Linguistic Code-Switching." *The Washington Post,* July 6, 2018.

Schmidt, Jennifer, Shankar Vedantam, Parth Shah, and Tara Boyle. "The Edge Effect." *Hidden Brain,* National Public Radio, July 3, 2018.

Tavernise, Sabrina. "Why the Announcement of a Looming White Minority Makes Demographers Nervous." *The New York Times,* November 22, 2018.

Tefera, Goshu Wolde. "Racial and Ethnic Identity Within the Ethiopian Diaspora in the United States and Their Political Engagement in Ethiopia: The Case of the Washington, D.C., Metropolitan Area." MA thesis, Syracuse University, 2016.

Vecchio, Diane. "Ties of Affection: Family Narratives in the History of Italian Migration." *Journal of American Ethnic History* 25, no. 2–3 (2006): 117–33.

Yang, Jeff. "'Fresh Off the Boat' and the Revolutionary Act of Kissing." *The Atlantic,* November 2, 2015.

BOOKS

Alinejad, Masih. *Wind in My Hair: My Fight for Freedom in Modern Iran.* Boston: Little, Brown, 2018.

Al Samawi, Mohammed. *The Fox Hunt: A Refugee's Memoir of Coming to America.* New York: HarperCollins, 2018.

Beah, Ishmael. *A Long Way Gone: Memoirs of a Boy Soldier.* New York: Farrar, Straus and Giroux, 2007.

Chua, Amy. *Battle Hymn of the Tiger Mother.* New York: Penguin Press, 2011.

Chua, Amy, and Jed Rubenfeld. *The Triple Package: How Three Unlikely Traits Explain the Rise and Fall of Cultural Groups in America.* New York: Penguin Books, 2015.

Cooper, Helene. *The House on Sugar Beach: In Search of a Lost African Childhood.* New York: Simon & Schuster, 2009.

Cornejo Villavicencio, Karla. *The Undocumented Americans.* New York: One World, 2020.

Danticat, Edwidge. *Brother, I'm Dying.* New York: Alfred A. Knopf, 2007.

DeParle, Jason. *A Good Provider Is One Who Leaves: One Family and Migration in the 21st Century.* New York: Viking, 2019.

Eggers, Dave. *What Is the What.* New York: Vintage, 2007.

Ferrera, America. *American Like Me: Reflections on Life Between Cultures.* New York: Gallery Books, 2018.

Fiss, Owen. *A Community of Equals.* Boston: Beacon Press, 1999.

Franklin, Benjamin. *The Papers of Benjamin Franklin,* vol. 4. Ed. by Leonard W. Labaree. New Haven, CT: Yale University Press, 1961.

Giridharadas, Anand. *The True American.* New York: W. W. Norton, 2014.

Gjelten, Tom. *A Nation of Nations.* New York: Simon & Schuster, 2015.

Golinkin, Lev. *A Backpack, a Bear, and Eight Crates of Vodka: A Memoir.* New York: Anchor, 2015.

Grande, Reyna. *The Distance Between Us: A Memoir.* New York: Simon & Schuster, 2013.

Guerrero, Diane. *In the Country We Love: My Family Divided.* New York: Henry Holt, 2018.

Handlin, Oscar. *The Uprooted: The Epic Story of the Great Migrations That Made the American People.* Boston: Little, Brown, 1951.

Hoffman, Eva. *Lost in Translation: A Life in a New Language.* New York: Penguin, 1990.

Holmes, Seth. *Fresh Fruit, Broken Bodies: Migrant Farmworkers in the United States.* Berkeley: University of California Press, 2013.

Iftin, Abdi Nor. *Call Me American: A Memoir.* New York: Alfred A. Knopf, 2018.

Kennedy, John F. *A Nation of Immigrants.* New York: Harper Perennial, 2008.

Khan, Khizr. *An American Family: A Memoir of Hope and Sacrifice.* New York: Random House, 2017.

Kidder, Tracy. *Strength in What Remains.* New York: Random House, 2010.

Kim, Joseph, and Stephan Talty. *Under the Same Sky: From Starvation in North Korea to Salvation in America.* Boston: Houghton Mifflin Harcourt, 2016.

Mehta, Suketu. *This Land Is Our Land: An Immigrant's Manifesto.* New York: Farrar, Straus and Giroux, 2019.

Metzker, Isaac, and Harry Golden. *A Bintel Brief: Sixty Years of Letters from the Lower East Side to the "Jewish Daily Forward."* New York: Schocken, 1990.

Nguyen, Viet Thanh. *The Displaced: Refugee Writers on Refugee Lives.* New York: Harry N. Abrams, 2018.

Park, Lisa Sun-Hee, and David N. Pellow. *The Slums of Aspen: Immigrants vs. the Environment in America's Eden.* New York: New York University Press, 2013.

Ramos, Jorge. *Stranger: The Challenge of a Latino Immigrant in the Trump Era.* New York: Vintage, 2018.

Schlesinger, Arthur M., Jr. *The Disuniting of America.* New York: W. W. Norton, 1992.

Shteyngart, Gary. *Little Failure.* New York: Random House, 2014.

Wamariya, Clemantine. *The Girl Who Smiled Beads: A Story of War and What Comes After.* New York: Crown, 2018.

Washington, George. *The Papers of George Washington,* vol. 6. Edited by W. W. Abbot. Charlottesville: University Press of Virginia, 1997.

Wilson, Woodrow, and Albert Bushnell Hart. *Selected Addresses and Public Papers of Woodrow Wilson.* New York: Boni and Liveright, 1918.

Yang, Wesley. *The Souls of Yellow Folk: Essays.* New York: W. W. Norton, 2018.

Zangwill, Israel. *The Melting Pot.* New York: The MacMillan Company, 1909.

GUIDEBOOKS

American Social Science Association. *Handbook for Immigrants to the United States.* 1871.

Benecke, Louis. *Handbook for Immigrants and Short Presentation of the Advantages Which Chariton County in the State of Missouri Offers to Immigrants.* Chariton County Society, 1873.

Brockett, L. P. *Handbook of the United States of America, 1880: A Guide to Emigration.* Old House Projects, 2014.

Goldberger, Henry. *English for Coming Citizens.* New York: Charles Scribner's Sons, 1918.

Hampshire, David. *Living and Working in America: A Survival Handbook.* Bath, UK: Survival Books, Ltd., 2008.

Keller, Frances. *Immigrants in America.* New York: Committee for Immigrants in America, 1915.

Kelly, Patrick. *Advice and Guide to Emigrants.* Dublin: William Folds, 1834.

MacLeod, Malcolm. *Practical Guide for Emigrants to the United States and Canada.* Manchester: A. Ireland, 1870.

Mikes, George. *How to Be an Alien.* London: Penguin UK, 1966.

O'Hanlon, John. *Reverend John O'Hanlon's The Irish Emigrant's Guide for the United States.* New York: Arno Press, 1976.

Razovsky, Cecilia. *What Every Emigrant Should Know.* New York: Council of Jewish Women, 1922.

Schibsby, Marian. *Handbook for Immigrants to the United States.* New York: Foreign Language Information Service, 1927.

A NOTE ABOUT THE AUTHOR

Roya Hakakian is the author of two books of poetry in Persian and two books of nonfiction in English, including the memoir *Journey from the Land of No: A Girlhood Caught in Revolutionary Iran.* A writing instructor at the THREAD at Yale, she is the recipient of a Guggenheim fellowship in nonfiction. She came to the United States as a refugee and is now a proud though concerned naturalized citizen.

A NOTE ON THE TYPE

This book was set in a modern adaptation of a type designed by the first William Caslon (1692–1766). The Caslon face, an artistic, easily read type, has enjoyed more than two centuries of popularity in our own country. It is of interest to note that the first copies of the Declaration of Independence and the first paper currency distributed to the citizens of the newborn nation were printed in this typeface.

Typeset by Scribe,
Philadelphia, Pennsylvania

Printed and bound by Berryville Graphics,
Berryville, Virginia